Conversations About The History of Ideas

Conversations About

THE HISTORY OF IDEAS

Edited by Howard Burton

Ideas Roadshow conversations present a wealth of candid insights from some of the world's leading experts, generated through a focused yet informal setting. They are explicitly designed to give non-specialists a uniquely accessible window into frontline research and scholarship that wouldn't otherwise be encountered through standard lectures and textbooks.

Over 100 Ideas Roadshow conversations have been held since our debut in 2012, covering a wide array of topics across the arts and sciences.

All Ideas Roadshow conversations are available both as part of a collection or as an individual eBook.

See www.ideasroadshow.com for a full listing of all titles.

Copyright ©2020 Open Agenda Publishing. All rights reserved.

ISBN: 978-1-77170-127-3 (pb)
ISBN: 978-1-77170-124-2 (eBook)

Edited, with preface and all introductions written by Howard Burton.

All *Ideas Roadshow Conversations* use Canadian spelling.

Contents

TEXTUAL NOTE 7

PREFACE 9

THE TWO CULTURES, REVISITED
A CONVERSATION WITH STEFAN COLLINI

Introduction 17
I. Cultural Assumptions 23
II. Saving the World 27
III. "Literary Osteoporosis" 30
IV. Into the Mainstream 33
V. Enter F.R. Leavis 36
VI. Combating Clichés 41
VII. The Fallout 45
VIII. Lessons Learned? 48
IX. What Are Universities For? 54
X. Constructive Engagement 59
XI. The Humanities vs. The Sciences 64
XII. General Implications 68
Continuing the Conversation 71

DECONSTRUCTING GENIUS
A CONVERSATION WITH DARRIN MCMAHON

Introduction 75
I. Opening Up Sightlines 80
II. The Equality Paradox 86
III. Towards The Dark Side 91
IV. Romantic Genius 95
V. Nature vs. Nurture 99
VI. Evil Genius 105
VII. Geniuses Everywhere 114
VIII. The Future of Genius 119
IX. Gradually Expanding 122
X. The Science of Genius 125
Continuing the Conversation 131

TURNING THE MIRROR
A VIEW FROM THE EAST
A CONVERSATION WITH PANKAJ MISHRA

    Introduction 135
    I. A Different Perspective 140
    II. Demanding a Response 144
    III. Inseparable Factors? 147
    IV. East and West 150
    V. Discovering Buddhism 156
    VI. Personal Examinations 161
    VII. At an Impasse 167
    VIII. Learning From the Past 171
    Continuing the Conversation 177

PANTS ON FIRE
ON LYING IN POLITICS
A CONVERSATION WITH MARTIN JAY

    Introduction 181
    I. A Fruitful Approach 186
    II. The Liar's Stage 190
    III. Lies, American Style 194
    IV. Transcending Kant 198
    V. Coming Clean 203
    VI. Monological Dangers 207
    VII. Democracy 211
    VIII. Getting Worse? 214
    IX. Puritanical Dangers 217
    X. Politics vs. Science 219
    XI. Summing Up 225
    Continuing the Conversation 229

QUEST FOR FREEDOM
A CONVERSATION WITH QUENTIN SKINNER

    Introduction 233
    I. Paradoxical Origins 238
    II. Presupposing the State 244
    III. The Perils of Arbitrary Power 248
    IV. Freedom, Applied 256
    V. Rhetoric 268
    VI. Reshaping a Moral World 276
    VII. Question and Answer 280
    Continuing the Conversation 287

Textual Note

The contents of this book are based upon separate filmed conversations with Howard Burton and each of the five featured experts.

Stefan Collini is Professor Emeritus of Intellectual History and English Literature at the University of Cambridge. This conversation occurred on April 19, 2013.

Darrin McMahon is the Mary Brinsmead Wheelock Professor of History at Dartmouth College. This conversation occurred on August 12, 2013.

Pankaj Mishra is an award-winning writer. This conversation occurred on March 21, 2013.

Martin Jay is the Sidney Hellman Ehrman Professor of History Emeritus at UC Berkeley. This conversation occurred on September 10, 2014.

Quentin Skinner is Barber Beaumont Professor of the Humanities at Queen Mary University of London. This conversation occurred on June 5, 2014.

Howard Burton is the creator and host of Ideas Roadshow and was Founding Executive Director of Perimeter Institute for Theoretical Physics.

Preface

Definitions are often thorny things to be dealing with, not infrequently raising nearly as many difficult questions as they were invented to deal with.

So it is with "intellectual history" or "the history of ideas". What does it mean, exactly, to be engaged in "the history of ideas"? It is hardly as simple as just coolly observing how a particular concept, like "genius" or "freedom", methodically unfolds down the ages like some curious sort of intellectual baton in a grand historical relay race.

Indeed, precisely those sorts of caricatures have oftentimes resulted in serious scholars beating a hasty retreat from anything that deigns to call itself "the history of ideas", as **Darrin McMahon** explains.

> "I was interested in intellectual history at a time when to do it was slightly looked askance at. And to do the history of ideas, in the way that I'm doing it now, really was taboo. There was a lot of good work done in the 60s and 70s that debunked an older approach to the history of ideas. The "great torch theory": the idea that one great thinker—Plato, say,—hands the torch to Aristotle and so on down the ages. That work seemed superficial, it seemed overly idealist in the philosophical sense, and it seemed removed from reality and the lives of ordinary people. So it was cast aside as no longer interesting.

> "But I'm trying to recover a type of history that takes on board many of the criticisms that have been levelled at the history of ideas—good criticisms—over the last several decades and yet recaptures this sense of the longue durée, recaptures some of the genuine excitement of the play of ideas over the ages. This kind of history of ideas does have the capacity to open up sightlines over the centuries that you

would miss if you didn't do it in this way. That's one of the things I find redeeming about this kind of work."

Another problem with establishing subdisciplinary boundaries—hardly limited to a topic like the history of ideas—is not only meaningfully describing what it *is*, but almost equally challenging, also what it is *not*.

After all, might it not be reasonably proposed that *every* historian who is diligently trying to rigorously interpret and investigate a given set of past events from their remote historical antecedents to their present-day implications is engaged in "the history of ideas"? How reasonable, then, is it to posit the existence of "non ideas-oriented historians"? Not very.

But that, I think, is not a terribly helpful point. Of course any serious, thoughtful historian—and in my experience most historians tend naturally to be serious, thoughtful types to begin with—will be strongly motivated to appreciate the prevailing ideas and beliefs of the period they are investigating and their consequent influence on the hearts and minds of their historical subjects, but what seems to set the history of ideas apart from other domains is a certain distinctiveness of approach, a determination to use historical investigation as a means to better appreciate and contextualize our current beliefs and attitudes.

And so you will find, in this collection, **Stefan Collini** returning to *The Two Cultures* "confrontation" between C.P. Snow and F.R. Leavis, not only deepening our historical awareness of the issues of the time well beyond a pat dichotomy between the "arts" and "sciences", but to better inform our present understanding of societal appeals to authority and celebrity culture; **Martin Jay** examining the intersection of lying and politics to demonstrate our perpetual conviction that things are getting worse, even as he probes the shifting boundaries of "the political"; **Quentin Skinner** methodically examining the implications of "arbitrary power" from Republican

Rome to Renaissance Florence to the contemporary government surveillance of emails.

There is, then, a common vein of harnessing a careful investigation of the past to better comprehend our present that runs through all of these conversations. Of course any editorial decision is to some extent arbitrary, and it clearly could be argued that I could have grouped things differently.

Why not include the conversation with **David Hollinger**, universally recognized to be one of America's greatest living intellectual historians? Surely the conversation about democracy with **John Dunn** would also fit within a collection dedicated to examining how a historical understanding of "big picture" concepts can enhance contemporary understanding, as would the conversation with **David Armitage** on Civil War.

Well, one has to draw the line somewhere.

But there is another point, too, that needs to be stressed, a driving aspect of what clearly motivates Quentin Skinner in his historico-philosophical inquiries. As important as it is to try to fully appreciate where our contemporary beliefs and values come from, that is not enough, because a properly rigorous study of the history of ideas not only sheds light on *why* we believe what we do, but what we might have **missed** along the way.

> "*We tend to write history as the history of the winners. We write the history of wars as the history of the winners, but we also write the history of our culture as the history of the winners. But did the winners always deserve to win? It's a huge question that historians ought to have at the forefront of their mind while working on anything which is a product of the human spirit and intelligence.*
>
> "*We've talked a lot today about a particular way of thinking about freedom, where I think that we're not the winners. We lost sight of something. And it's quite easy to provide strong historical explanations of why we lost sight of a particular way of thinking about freedom and citizenship, but I've come to think that it is deeper and*

> more powerful than what we've currently got on offer. So we ought to be recovering it, we ought to treat it as buried treasure, we ought to be bringing it to the surface, dusting it down.
>
> "And once you begin to doubt our way of thinking about freedom, which I do, you'd start to doubt other things, because many of these terms are interconnected and inter-defined. You'd start to think differently about rights. You'd start to think differently about equality.
>
> "So you begin to reshape a moral world for yourself. You're not, of course, replicating a past moral world. You're taking elements from that world which you might not have thought about and are trying to reinsert them into our world. And I've come to think that that's a very important part of the intellectual historian's task."

And here, finally, is why the conversation with **Pankaj Mishra** is included in this collection.

Pankaj, of course, is not even a professional historian, let alone a professional "intellectual historian", but his captivating book on which much of our conversation was based, *From the Ruins of Asia: The Intellectuals Who Remade Asia*, is very much in the tradition of Quentin Skinner's expressed desire to "recover buried treasure".

And in my view, the very fact that Pankaj is not a career academic but a bestselling writer intent on directly influencing his surrounding society as strongly as he can, only emphasizes the enormous relevance of the history of ideas for all of us.

> "As a writer, I feel my responsibility is to point people to particular aspects of our past which have not been written about, which have been ignored and neglected, and to encourage them to explore those aspects much, much deeper. The important thing is that all our histories, whether you're in the West or in the East, are full of instances of journeys not taken, roads not taken, alternative modernities never really explored.
>
> "It's important to develop a historical awareness that, This is also how people once lived upon this earth: they were also violent, they were also greedy and selfish, but they devised certain political and

economical mechanisms whereby those negative tendencies could be controlled and contained and the damage from them could be limited.

"That is what I, in my own very modest way, am trying to do: to point to particular instances of this—or even just to people who talked about those particular instances—and say, "Well, we just can't stand here today and say there is no alternative but to go down this path of collective suicide and destruction of the planet".

"We just can't do that. That would be the worst kind of intellectual dishonesty, because there have been human societies before us, centuries and centuries of them, with their own ways of being, with their own ways of living.

"And this is what, I think, as a writer, I can do: I can simply point to them."

The Two Cultures, Revisited

A conversation with Stefan Collini

Introduction

Returning to the Source

In what surely must rank as the acme of literary reviews, *The Observer* once famously remarked that Eric Hobsbawm's comprehensive historical tetralogy on "the long 19th century" had become "*part of the mental furniture of educated Englishmen*".

The French have an expression for such a thing: *culture générale*. This carries a decidedly different semantic hue than our rather more pedestrian "common knowledge". After all, common knowledge is what everybody is supposed to possess just by living in the world around them, while *culture générale* is what a cultivated person should have at her fingertips, the hard-earned result of a solid, well-rounded education that will enable the well-educated soul to make sense of the world around her.

But sometimes this goes awry, as it occasionally happens that by the time an idea has worked its way into the public consciousness, the context has been hallowed out into little more than a misleading cliché.

So it was, for me at least, with *The Two Cultures*, the celebrated phrase that originated in the 1959 Rede Lecture that C.P. Snow gave at the University of Cambridge.

I thought I knew what *The Two Cultures* was all about. Indeed, during my time spent as an evangelical academic administrator, I had quite often explicitly invoked its core message of the need to somehow bridge the increasing gap between the sciences and the humanities so that they can both sufficiently flower.

The trouble was, however, that this wasn't actually the core message of the work at all, a state of affairs that I was happily unaware of since, like most who now glibly refer to *The Two Cultures*, I had never actually taken the time to read Snow's lecture. Nor, as it happens, did I know anything about the famously acerbic attack that his principal antagonist, F.R. Leavis, launched against him three years later.

Which was a real shame. Not just because an unread text is a dangerously shaky foundation upon which to build an argument (which is certainly true), but also because the famously tempestuous exchange between Leavis and Snow still has much to teach the reflective observer more than fifty years later.

University of Cambridge literary critic and intellectual historian Stefan Collini, suffice it to say, has studied the exchange in considerable detail, supplying thoughtful and comprehensive introductions to the recently reissued texts of both Snow's 1959 lecture and Leavis' 1962 response.

So what was it actually all about?

> *"I think what Snow was most animated by was the thought that the application of technology to bettering the world is going to become more and more important: to feeding those in the less prosperous parts of the world, to developing the economies of the more prosperous parts of the world and so on.*
>
> *"And he was very concerned that the people who were in a position of influence and power in Britain—not just in Britain, elsewhere as well, but he mainly concentrates on Britain in that lecture—were, by and large in his view, not scientifically trained, not really familiar enough with the possible benefits of science and how scientific thinking worked. And so he believed that many of the advantages of the use of science and technology were just not going to be realized, that people who were ignorant of them were going to be making the wrong sorts of decisions."*

Well, that seems unproblematic enough, if admittedly a far cry from the typical arts vs. science academic battlefield that I had long imagined that *The Two Cultures* represented. But what on earth could have possibly provoked F.R. Leavis to respond to this so aggressively? And who was Leavis anyway?

> *"Leavis was a particular kind of literary critic. He passionately believed in the power of great literature to open up our world and our experience if read sufficiently attentively and with the kind of disciplined attention that an education in English literature could give you.*

> *"But he didn't believe in the kind of scholarly apparatus, the over-emphasis on knowledge about the biographical or contextual details. He believed very much in the personal response to it, if it was of the right disciplined kind. He had become a really quite fearsome controversialist, because he always wanted to press anybody he engaged with, "What do **you** really believe? How do you **respond** to this?"*

> *"So then he read this lecture by Snow, and he was appalled. He was appalled, first of all, because he thought that the uptake of Snow, the success that the lecture had, showed how devalued and empty a lot of the categories of public acceptance really were. If people thought that **this** was a serious analysis of a serious problem, in other words, then we're in trouble."*

But for Leavis, it was much more than simply a matter of taking Snow to task over his pompous and superficial style. What really infuriated him was Snow's banal and uncritical reduction of the aims of human life to nothing more than mere economic self-sufficiency.

> *"What people don't remember about Leavis' attack is that it was not just a personal attack on Snow, or even on Snow's reputation. Leavis, too, is fundamentally preoccupied with what we as a society posit as the ends of human life. What are the values and purposes we should really be striving for?*

> *"He says, 'The picture you get from Snow's lecture about this is really a kind of empty prosperity.' He picks up a phrase that Snow uses rather lightly in his own lecture: the only goal is 'jam today*

and more jam tomorrow'— a kind of vacuous prosperity that has got no sense of what's worthwhile, what's really a human form of flourishing. And he maintains that Snow is complicit in this, that Snow is endorsing this."

We find ourselves, suddenly, a long, long, way from the question of whether or not undergraduate humanities students should be forced to take a "Physics for Poets" course as part of their standard curriculum.

We are also, as it happens, squarely in Stefan Collini's wheelhouse. For Stefan is not only a trenchant intellectual historian, he is also a passionate advocate for critical public engagement on a number of pressing societal issues, with many deeply penetrating views of his own.

His book, *What Are Universities For?* for example, is a careful examination of what academe is and what it might become, a passionate urging, à la F.R. Leavis, for all of us to exercise our critical faculties, albeit expressed in much less vitriolic prose.

"The thing is not looked at very closely, but there is a strong sense among the policy-making, administrative and media classes that the only thing that's really going to justify public support in whatever form for universities, the only thing that will do that is economic growth.

"And what we get are these unexamined assumptions imported wholesale from not even really the active business world—they're not what some of the best businessmen and top financiers would say about their own activities—but the kind of second-hand reporting of, and perception of, what is business-like about business. We get those clichés and categories imported into the judging and assessing of universities in ways that don't capture what universities are so good at.

"This is why I tried to start where I did, in working towards finding a language that can express that accountability and answerability adequately. We've got to do something more than see universities as *either a glorified apprenticeship scheme in which we train people for particular, specified jobs in industry, or as some kind of industrial lab, in which we come up with inventions that will make products that can be sold or cure some disease.*

"Rather than saying that universities have no responsibility to society or universities don't contribute to the benefit of society, I want to say that unless we allow them the freedom to do what they're really good at we will lose the benefit to society that they give."

And so he continues, carefully examining the nuance of language in the same meticulous spirit of critical inquiry that F.R. Leavis held so dear.

Stefan's commentary is hardly the sort of thing I might have imagined would flow naturally from a re-examination of *The Two Cultures* debate. But then, once you get beyond misleading stereotypes and start paying close attention to what was actually said and why, all sorts of interesting connections start falling into place.

The Conversation

I. Cultural Assumptions
On the benefits of reading

HB: Let me start with a candid admission. A few months ago I had never heard of F.R. Leavis. I *had* heard of C.P. Snow, and *The Two Cultures*, but the truth was that I only realized later that I knew even less about where that phrase came from than I thought I did.

Which brings to mind a funny story that led to me contacting you. I was in a book store about 9 months ago and spotted a copy of *The Two Cultures*—the Canto edition with your Introduction.

And I thought to myself, I should probably read this because this is one of those canonical phrases that I've not only heard of, but also used, and I should learn about the historical details. But then I felt overcome by almost a sense of embarrassment—I'm not sure if you've ever felt this way—but my sense was that this is so much a part of general culture that at some level I felt I should already know all about it and so I shouldn't have to buy it.

SC: It's like going up to the counter and asking, *"Do you have a book called War and Peace?"*

HB: Exactly. And so I had this little battle with myself and I eventually concluded that I was just being silly. I was pretty sure that I hadn't actually read it before, so I should take the opportunity to buy it and read it.

And when I went to the cash to pay, the fellow at the cash looked down at my purchase and said, *"Oh, C.P. Snow and The Two Cultures. Do you think it's just as relevant today as it was when he wrote it?"*

And I replied, *"Well, actually, I've never read it, you see. That's why I'm buying it."* And then he turned to me and admitted, *"I've never read it either."*

That gave me a sense of how much this phrase has permeated the public consciousness. Many people are aware of the fact that C.P. Snow said some things about "two cultures", about the growing gulf between the humanities and the sciences, but that's really as far as it goes.

So let's start off with the basics. What actually happened? Who was C.P. Snow, and what did he actually say?

SC: What I liked about your story was that the man at the cash had the assumption that you could have quite an interesting conversation about this even though neither of you had read it. And I think that's partially because the phrase has come to stand for a set of issues: even people who've never read Snow's actual text think that there is something quite interesting here. Maybe they think it's to do with the place of science in our culture, or maybe they think it's got something do with how we should organize education, but they're willing to be engaged just by the phrase, without even having read the thing itself.

But let's go back a bit, as you suggest, and give a sense of what he was really saying.

It might be helpful if at first I just say a word or two about how Snow got to this point. Snow trained originally as a research scientist, as a chemist, and his scientific career was not altogether successful. He had one or two setbacks, he claimed some discovery that didn't quite stand up, and he progressively moved towards administration.

When the Second World War started he began recruiting scientists for government service, and then after the war he carried on recruiting them for the civil service. At the same time, through the 1930s and into the 1940s and 1950s, he was writing novels very successfully.

So when he got invited in 1959 to give this high-profile lecture at Cambridge, he already had quite a reputation as a novelist, he was known to be somebody who was a trained scientist—in fact he was thought to have a bit more of a scientific reputation and standing than he really did have, he hadn't been a practicing scientist for some time—but he certainly came from that background.

And so he was able to set himself up as, if you like, having a foot in both camps; or at least being an authority about these things in a way that not so many people could. That, I think, is one crucial thing that led to the success and the amount of attention that this lecture got.

I think what Snow was most animated by was the thought that the application of technology to bettering the world is going to become more and more important: to feeding those in the less prosperous parts of the world, to developing the economies of the more prosperous parts of the world, and so on.

And he was very concerned that the people who were in a position of influence and power in Britain—not just in Britain, elsewhere as well, but he mainly concentrates on Britain in that lecture—were, by and large in his view, not scientifically trained, not really familiar enough with the possible benefits of science and how scientific thinking worked. And so he believed that many of the advantages of the use of science and technology were just not going to be realized, that people who were ignorant of them were going to be making the wrong sorts of decisions.

HB: And not only that the advantages wouldn't be realized, but that scientific thinking was even sometimes being scorned by those in power.

SC: Well, that's the thing. Because he then says that what's happened here is that we've had two cultures grow up, really: those who are educated in what he calls the 'traditional literary culture' who are often those who became the most influential and achieved positions of power. I should say that we could take issue with that: that's not necessarily very accurate about Britain, or the United States for that matter, in the 1950s. But we can come back to that.

He saw the literary formation as the traditional dominant culture, and then over here were all those who were trained in science. And the evaluation, in society at large, was that the literary culture was somehow "Culture" with a capital C: it was respectable and was something that people could aspire to and look up to. Meanwhile, the scientific culture, according to Snow, was looked down upon a bit, it was viewed as being somehow slightly shabby and utilitarian.

And one of the impulses, I think, in this famous lecture is to assert the standing and the importance for the future of the world, of science and technology—not just in intellectual terms, but in terms of global social and economic development: to minimize, if not to overcome, what he saw as this damaging divide.

I think that's a reasonably accurate and fair account. I think you'd have to say, as you read the lecture more closely, that he actually wants to assert the priority of the scientific culture over the literary culture. It's not so even-handed as all that.

Questions for Discussion:

1. Have you heard of the phrase "The Two Cultures"? Have you read Snow's lecture?

2. What do you think of when you hear the word "culture"? Is science part of "culture"?

II. Saving the World
C.P. Snow's moral agenda

HB: Even before we get there, he does make this illustrative comment exactly along the lines of what you're saying: rhetorically asking how many among us are able to demonstrate any real awareness of the second law of thermodynamics, a rough scientific equivalent in his view to being familiar with the works of Shakespeare.

And my sense is that, it is *that* aspect of *The Two Cultures* that pervades the public consciousness. What is *The Two Cultures* about? Well, we have the humanities and we have the sciences, and for far too long the humanities were considered more important and the natural home for a fully capable and intellectual dynamic individual, while the scientists were just these geeky, number-crunching people who could carry out various necessary, as you say utilitarian, calculations, but weren't really all that impressive or cultured in the broad, general sense of things.

So that part I expected. But what you mentioned just now: the overwhelming importance of science for the explicit betterment of humanity, that was something that completely floored me when I read it, because I had no awareness that it had been talked about at all during this lecture, and it seemed to be a very major theme indeed.

SC: Right. If we go back to your man at the cash at the bookshop, had you asked him, *"Well, what do you think Snow said?"*, I think it's fair to say that he would never have mentioned this question of social and economic development.

HB: Absolutely not. Nor would I have, for that matter.

SC: So that's why I say that a set of associations have grown up, a set of assumptions of what *The Two Cultures* stand for that focuses almost entirely on this matter of the educational arrangements and then the social evaluations of the two casts of mind, or two forms of practice.

But when you read the lecture, as you said, and especially when you get towards the end, once he has set up this account of the divide, what he then really focuses in on is what's going to happen to the world. In some ways he draws a parallel between the benefits that came to what then became the developed world through the Industrial Revolution in the late 18th and early 19th centuries and the benefits that could now come to the undeveloped world if the most recent forms of technology could be fully exploited to develop industry and agriculture in those places.

In a way, then, I think that the lecture is 'end-driven': that's the state he wants to get to, the diagnosis is of what's holding it back.

HB: There are two things that are interesting to me about these views expressed by Snow in the 1950s. The first is, as you wrote in your Introduction, the assumption that bettering mankind was a necessary activity: it wasn't a question of *whether* we should help people in the poorer parts of the world, it was a question of *how* we should do it.

SC: Right.

HB: And the second noteworthy thing, at least to me, is Snow's belief that those who didn't have a proper scientific orientation would not be helpful in contributing to this mission, or at least in not the best possible way.

Questions for Discussion:

1. Do you think that **The Two Cultures** *theme has a particular relevance for environmental issues?*

2. Do the views about science expressed in this chapter confuse "science" with "technology"? If so, to what extent do we make the same mistake today?

III. "Literary Osteoporosis"
Scientists vs. "literary intellectuals"

HB: Let's get back to this notion of scientific triumphalism where I cut you off before. It is clear that Snow wants to align himself with the scientists and distance himself from what he dubbed the "literary intellectuals", calling them Luddites and all the rest. This is curious because, as you said, it seemed like at the time that he was seen by the great majority of people as more on the literary side of things than he was on the scientific side of things.

SC: Well, the first thing I would say is that people think that *The Two Cultures* talks about the divide between the sciences and what we generally call the humanities, thinking about that in mainly university terms, perhaps. It's interesting, because Snow doesn't really set it up like that.

His other group is, as you said, the "literary intellectuals". The examples are nearly always novelists or poets, not scholars in universities. And it is only literature—that is, not historians or philosophers or the students of ancient languages and so on. It's not that side of things that he's talking about.

And that, I think, in some ways makes his case much less persuasive, because the idea that the so-called dominant elites in British society in the middle of the 20th century are making their decisions because they've been formed by reading things by D.H. Lawrence or T.S. Eliot or whatever, well, it just doesn't really look that way.

You can say, *"Yes, often these were people who went to Oxford or Cambridge and did classics or English or history".* That may be true: they didn't study science and may be a bit underinformed about that.

But his picture of what is so damaging or backward-looking about the literary culture is framed around examples from writers, and a particular generation of writers too. It's what people call The High Modernist generation, the writers who came to prominence in the 1910s–1930s and who often famously had very conservative, reactionary, sometimes even quasi-fascist political affiliations.

So Snow was able to say, *"Look, these people point us in a terrible direction. This is what's so backward-looking about the literary culture."* And then he slides over and says, *"This represents the traditional culture"*, before explicitly contrasting it with his evaluation of the scientific culture. You remember the famous phrase: *"The scientists have the future in their bones."* They're forward-looking, they are positive about the prospects for humanity, whereas these literary intellectuals, the reason they are Luddites is not just that they're ignorant but because they actually actively resist.

HB: They have the past in their bones.

SC: Yes, exactly. They've got osteoporosis of a kind.

HB: At some point Snow mentions a conversation he had some years before with the famous mathematician G.H. Hardy where Hardy muses that the word 'intellectual' is being thrown around an awful lot, but it didn't seem to include people like him. And it seems to me that that's still very much true today.

If one hears the word "intellectual", the image that comes to mind is not a chemist or a mathematician. One can imagine a certain degree of offense being taken by scientists or mathematicians when it comes to this. So maybe Snow is reflecting a common concern within the scientific community here: it's not just his own perspective, perhaps there is some ground swell of resistance that's coming through.

SC: The first thing that I would say is that being called an intellectual is not always a desirable thing in British culture at that time. The scientists might think they got off lightly in this respect.

The other thing I would say is that that's broadly right, as you put it there. But if you look just slightly more closely, a lot of the figures who engaged in public debate in some way from a position of cultural authority in those middle decades of the 20th century were, in fact, scientists. If we think of people like J.D. Bernal or J.B.S. Haldane or Peter Medawar, these were all scientists who had a voice in public debate and had a lot of what we would now call media exposure.

I think that, very often, Snow puts his thumb on the scale a bit to accentuate the contrast, but broadly speaking I think you're right. He is voicing something that a lot of ordinary, practicing scientists at the time would have felt: both that what they did was a little derogated or looked down upon in some way, and—even if they wouldn't always make this entirely explicit—that what they did was in some way more reliable knowledge, more exact and more useful. I think Snow is giving voice to that cluster of feelings.

HB: And "more useful" not only for the people in that particular society but "more useful" broad brush, on a planetary level.

SC: That's right. For humanity

Questions for Discussion:

1. To what extent do you think that Snow's focus on The High Modernist generation was related to his profession as a novelist?

2. What does it mean to be "an intellectual" today? Is it a positive term?

IV. Into the Mainstream
Snow becomes a sage

HB: So he gives this talk in 1959 and then what happens? How is it received? What sort of effect does it have?

SC: Well, one thing that happens is that it's received internationally. In the lecture itself he makes quite a few international references: he tells how he's been to Russia and seen what they're doing there as well as what's happening in the United States. It's important to remember that these are the Sputnik years where the sense of international scientific competition cum collaboration is quite a hot issue.

The lecture is taken up—not just in Britain but all over the world—as the announcement of a theme of real consequence for the future of the planet. Here's somebody who's pointing to an aspect of our cultural arrangements, especially our educational arrangements, which may, in some ways, be holding us back.

It wasn't that everybody was favourable about it—there were certainly critics—but I think the broad picture would be to say that in the few years immediately after it was given in 1959 it helped to project Snow into the position of being something of a sage or prophet whose opinions on everything were very eagerly solicited.

As I said earlier, the fact that he was known to be a successful novelist and a trained scientist added to his authority. People didn't look too closely at that but they thought, *"Here's somebody who knows both worlds very well and is in high level administration, he understands politics and knows about running things, and he is pointing to a real problem here"*. I think that was probably the single most dominant and positive form of reaction to it.

HB: And what happened in terms of acceptance of the ideas within the academic structure? Was there any motivation to change teaching methodology or curricula in any concrete way? Was there a clear desire to enfold or give more credence to some of these aspects of what he was saying in terms of changing the educational structure of Britain?

SC: Well, he's not saying something that it is wholly distinctive: he's picking up themes here that others have been saying.

Britain had, and still has, a more specialized secondary education system than many countries—much more than the United States, for example. British students in their last two or three years at high school may narrow down the study of only some humanities disciplines, or only some science disciplines, and then when they go to university they will more or less exclusively study just one of these. In addressing the arrangements in Britain he's addressing one of the most specialized educational systems in the world; and of course because it's been so specialized it's generated a lot of anxiety and reflection on whether this is desirable or whether it should be changed. That was already going on, and Snow gave it a very big push.

But the early 1960s was a time of a whole wave of new universities that were founded in Britain, a great expansion of the system. It was the kind of expansion that happened a bit earlier in the United States, in the years that happened after 1945, but didn't happen in Britain until the early 1960s. One of the things that was taken up in those new universities was the hope—not just from Snow, but often Snow was cited—that there would be a way for the curriculum to allow people who were going to specialize in science to do a bit of work in the humanities and vice versa. Quite a few universities in that period set up courses like this. In fact, my first teaching job was at the University of Sussex, which was one of these new universities.

When I went to Sussex in 1974, there was still something called the Arts-Science scheme, which was an attempt to get all students who were in the sciences to do some course from the humanities side of the university and vice versa. It was, I have to say, even then on its last legs. It was quite hard to get people to teach it, the pressure of professionalization and specialization told against it, and students quite often were a bit resistant to it, they saw it as just some sort of extra obligation.

HB: This was just for first year students, presumably? "Physics for poets" as we would say, or something like that.

SC: Yes, something like that. But it was very hard to make it work against the grain of the institution as a whole where people were either studying one subject or were specialists in teaching one subject. To go back to your question, I think that Snow gave a push to attempts to tinker with the basic structure, but I don't think that in the long term it really had much effect in changing that structure.

Questions for Discussion:

1. Do you think that students are forced to specialize in their studies too early? Not early enough?

2. What are the negative aspects of a deliberately "interdisciplinary" educational system?

V. Enter F.R. Leavis
Questioning authority

HB: So C.P. Snow gives this lecture. It's generally very well received and certainly in line with at least some of what the thinking is at the time. And then a few years later, along comes someone else with a rather different perspective on things.

SC: Yes. Enter, stage left, F.R. Leavis. Leavis was a literary critic. He'd spent his whole career teaching at Cambridge and did not respond to Snow's lecture when it was given, nor when it was published. But in 1962, three years after Snow's lecture, Leavis was himself invited to give another named lecture in Cambridge. And he decided that the time had come to take the measure of what was by then becoming really quite an influential statement by Snow.

I suppose it's important to say that Leavis was a particular kind of literary critic. He passionately believed in the power of great literature to open up our world and our experience if read sufficiently attentively and with the kind of disciplined attention that an education in English literature could give you.

But he didn't believe in the kind of scholarly apparatus, the over-emphasis on knowledge about the biographical or contextual details. He believed very much in the personal response to it, if it was of the right disciplined kind. He had become a really quite fearsome controversialist, because he always wanted to press anybody he engaged with, *"What do **you** really believe? How do **you** respond to this?"*

And he could do so with a good deal of belligerence. He was, himself, by then, something of a semi-public figure. He was quite well known, not as well known as Snow, but he was known beyond academia, certainly.

So then he read this lecture by Snow, and he was appalled. He was appalled, first of all, because he thought that the uptake of Snow, the success that the lecture had, showed how devalued and empty a lot of the categories of public acceptance really were. If people thought that **this** was a serious analysis of a serious problem, in other words, then we're in trouble.

In his own lecture, as you know, he unsparingly points out ways in which he thinks Snow's evaluation is vacuous, how a lot of it is second or third-rate; and he wants to say, *"What about this reputation and status that Snow has? How deserved is it? Snow is a **novelist!**"*

Leavis can barely contain himself at this point. The novels, he thinks, are just hopeless. They've got this unspeakable dialogue and all these clunky stage directions. He's not somebody who really understands the imaginative power of fiction. What he does instead is simply give you this low-grade social narrative. And so on.

And then he moves to the scientific perspective. Is Snow really bringing the voice of science to bear here? Well, of course, Leavis himself is not a trained and informed scientist, but he says, *"I think scientific thinking is marked by its rigour, its precision, its power. Do I see that in Snow's lecture? No: a lot of clichés, a lot of slack reasoning"* and so on.

So he completely savages, as it were, Snow's standing, his claim to do this.

But just as people don't remember that Snow's lecture was driven by the concern with some kind of human betterment through the application of technology, what people don't remember about Leavis' attack is that it was not just a personal attack on Snow, or even on Snow's reputation. Leavis, too, is fundamentally preoccupied with what we as a society posit as the ends of human life. What are the values and purposes we should really be striving for?

He says, *"The picture you get from Snow's lecture about this is really a kind of empty prosperity."* He picks up a phrase that Snow uses rather lightly in his own lecture: the only goal is jam today and more jam tomorrow, a kind of vacuous prosperity that has got no sense of what's worthwhile, what's really a human form of flourishing. And he maintains that Snow is complicit in this, that Snow is endorsing this.

HB: Wholeheartedly, in fact.

SC: Yes, wholeheartedly. He's pushing it. And that it is the dominant set of values of our public culture. So Leavis, as always—this is a feature of Leavis' writing more generally, but very much in this exchange—sets himself up as someone who is taking on this powerful, established discourse.

This is how politics, media, and our society more generally talk, these are the values that are set up for public admiration; and I, Leavis, am trying to call us back to a truer sense of what really matters. Where will we find that? Well, fundamentally, our best guides are going to be in the great writers.

He's not, as some people think, saying that education should only be in the humanities, and the sciences don't matter. He's actually, in some respects, very respectful of "real science", what he thinks of as good scientists doing good science. What he's not respectful of is somebody pontificating, on the basis of an association with science, about the importance of science over literature.

In that way he is fighting back on literature's behalf, but not in order to eliminate science by any means, but in order to find somewhere where we can look to find some kind of stimulus and guidance about how to think about living.

HB: As you were talking, there were two things that came to my mind. The first is that, as you alluded to earlier, Leavis casts aspersions not only on Snow's ability as a novelist, for which he is eminently qualified to do as a literary critic, but also his scientific credentials.

These, as you mentioned at the beginning, turned out to be quite a bit murkier than one might originally have believed: Snow left science rather precipitously and there was some sort of scandal that he was involved in. It wasn't as if he wilfully gave up this great, glorious, shining scientific future to become a literary figure because he could do so many things at the same time, but rather that he adjusted his career path more out of necessity due to circumstances.

So there was that. But to me, all of this is related to the deeper question of what an authority figure actually is, why society feels compelled to regard some people in this uncritical, unflinchingly positive light simply because they are, effectively, told to do so: some individual is brought in as an authority figure and given a platform to make grand utterances and be treated as a sage.

And so, although Leavis' attacks are shockingly vitriolic and unsparing—which makes for fantastically interesting reading by the way—

SC: Yes. It's very good fun in that way.

HB:—there is also clearly a sense that he's not just having a go at Snow because he wants to rip this particular fellow apart. He wants to rip apart the whole idea of intuitively trusting authority figures that are somehow thrust upon the public. He wants the public to be much more critical in their assessment of why such people are in a position to make such grand pronouncements in the first place.

SC. Yes, that's right. In fact, in Leavis' construction of it, this is a sort of vicious circle: somebody like Snow is made an authority figure in part because he gives society back the clichés that it wants to hear. And where does society get these clichés from? Well, they grow up in accumulation from these authority figures who have articulated them in the first place.

So in Leavis' view, somebody who is offering something that doesn't fit in so well with this, something that may be very antagonistic to the dominant conception and values of the society, is probably not going to be made into a sage, an authority figure, in the first place. There are only certain convenient voices.

Now I'd have to say, looking from the outside, that I think Leavis overstates that a bit. The world of public debate is more varied than that, as, in fact, Leavis himself showed. He, by any measure, got a hearing—

HB:—because of his reputation—

SC: Well, because of his reputation, and because of the intrinsic power of what he had to say. He wasn't just articulating the platitudes of the time, but a lot of people read him, and quite a lot saw that there was some force to what he had to say.

So I think he overstates that a bit. But you're absolutely right that his real preoccupation with that bit of the lecture is that the mechanism by which somebody gets this kind of celebrity status as a sage is what we need to undermine in some way. It's no good just saying, *"I disagree"*. It's no good even just saying, *"I, in general, disagree with C.P. Snow"*. You've got to somehow take the podium away from under him so he doesn't have the right to stand on it.

HB: He shouldn't have had such a podium to begin with.

SC: Yes. There shouldn't be such a podium.

Questions for Discussion:

1. Is the "vicious circle" of authority Leavis worries about worse today than it was in 1959?

2. Is the creation of public authority figures a necessary component of being human? Do some societies rely less on such authority figures than others?

VI. Combating Clichés
The Industrial Revolution and challenging prose

HB: Again, going back to the naive bookseller, or the naive book-purchaser, who thinks, *Ah, yes, C.P. Snow, The Two Cultures: the arts and the sciences should listen to each other more and there really shouldn't be this divide.* And perhaps an aspect of, science is more important than it's been generally recognized to be.

Now, instead, we're faced with something like:

Well, actually, one of Snow's central theses was this notion that science is vital to improving the prosperity of mankind. If we ignore, in our educational practices and overall assessments, this wonderful impact that science can have, we do so at our peril as well as at the peril of millions of people across the globe who need so much technological and practical assistance from us, because this is a key way to improve prosperity.

And on the other hand we have Leavis who, notwithstanding his reputation as the author of a vicious, ad hominem attack, is really focused on the idea that we should be regarding societal triumph in more than mere dry economic indicators while warning us of the inherent dangers of "celebrity culture" and elevating people to positions of public authority far too quickly and uncritically. These are two messages that are very different indeed from what your naive book-purchaser or book-seller might have had.

SC: That's right. In fact, as you know, the Leavis lecture is even less about that traditional notion of *The Two Cultures* than is Snow's: there's very little in there about educational arrangements and how to deal with that at all.

And the account you've just given is spot on, I think. One of the ways that's focused on is in Snow and Leavis' different evaluation of, and response to, the whole question of the Industrial Revolution.

In Snow, as we said earlier, the Industrial Revolution is really the first stage in which the exploitation of science and technology starts to give these societies lift-off towards prosperity. Snow gives a very positive account of the whole history. He says something like, *"Wherever the poor are being given the chance, they've walked off the land and into the factories; and that's their route to a better life."* It's true that when you reread Snow there is something very blandly optimistic about this: it does look like just "more jam tomorrow", it's true. And that's what Leavis hones in on.

Leavis doesn't deny that technology is hugely important. He doesn't deny that prosperity has its benefits for us. But he says, *"Well, wait. Is it really the case that the Industrial Revolution, in its first phase, was so unproblematically a benefit? It brought untold dislocations and suffering, and it surely also was part of what made the idea of prosperity seem like the only, or the overriding, goal that societies should pursue. The more things take off in that direction, the more other values are in some way disregarded."*

And again, Leavis makes the characteristic move of saying, *"Well, who diagnosed this? Who understood that this route of prosperity was more complicated, and that there were losses as well as gains?"*

And of course it was the novelists and the literary figures who were critics of this. People like Dickens, Carlyle or Matthew Arnold.

I think it's quite difficult to get Leavis' position clear because he's certainly not saying that he's against progress or against science altogether. He's not saying that. But he's saying that we're getting to the stage where we find it almost hard to articulate some set of values that will be persuasive in the public world other than increased prosperity.

We're getting so far along this road, and one of the ways to complicate our thinking about this and improve our public discourse would be to go back to the critics of industrialism and see what it is that they, at the time rather prophetically, saw were going to be some of the narrowing of human horizons and some of the very instrumental ways of thinking that were going to come out of this and do better about avoiding those sorts of pitfalls now.

In a way, not only are both these lectures more about economic progress and those large issues than the book-buyer and the book-seller thought they were, but they're also both more about history. They're more about contesting the story of progress in the last 200 years.

HB: In your Introduction to the book, you talk specifically about how aspects of Leavis' prose were received. There were people who commented on the fact that his writing was sometimes difficult to parse, that it was at times far too convoluted; there were critical remarks levelled not just at what he was saying but the manner in which he was expressing it.

I took this as a sign of Leavis' ongoing battle against triteness and simplification. As a literary critic and as somebody who was steeped in the tradition of English literature and believed in its power, he chose his words extremely carefully.

My impression was that what Leavis was effectively saying was, *"Well, this jolly well should be difficult to read: you have to make an effort to read this. It's not just one bland, pat phrase after another; and an essential aspect of genuine critical engagement requires that one goes slowly and makes a deliberate attempt to parse things, being diligent not only as a writer but also as a reader."*

SC: That's absolutely right. He says that you don't combat the power of cliché in our culture by replacing one cliché with another. Or as we might say now, you don't combat the power of sound bites just by another sound bite. What you need to do is, in some way, offer another kind of discourse—which, as you summarized it, will slow things down a bit, bring out the complexity, allow for a certain amount of uncertainty and have a prose that makes the reader think through the reading, not just receive it in some passive way.

It's true of Leavis' writing that it's often got that sinewy, but highly charged and slightly convoluted sense of there being a lot packed into a sentence. It's very rarely just subject—verb—object. It's subject (but the subject is this)—verb (of course when that)—adverb—adverb and then a whole proliferation of sub-clauses about the object. Leavis says at one point—he's very self-conscious about this—*"Oh, I know people charge that I write badly."*

But as you say, it wasn't that he wrote carelessly in the least. What he thought he was doing was trying, in a sense, to bring the reader up short: make the reader lose that easy assimilation of just taking in things with only half an eye or half an ear so that you find yourself having to do more thinking when you read him, and perhaps as a result become less susceptible to being taken in by the glib phrases and the things that are oversimplified because you've had your receptors, as it were, opened up a bit by this more complicated kind of prose.

His own writing does that; and then, of course, his usual message is that one of the ways in which we can help to cultivate this and, to some extent, train people to read and think better is by reading good writing, not just by reading the clichés of the daily press or of the politicians' speeches.

Once again, we come back to the importance of an education in literature.

Questions for Discussion:

1. To what extent do you believe that it is still the case today that the hard questions about the meaning of "societal progress" typically fall to the writers?

2. Is it possible for something to be written "too smoothly"?

VII. The Fallout
Immediate and longer-term effects

HB: So let's get back to the story. Leavis says all this in 1962, and then what happens? How is this received?

SC: What happens is that a great mountain of garbage is poured upon his head, really. That is to say that he's thought to be immensely offensive. You mentioned the rather personal aspects of the attack on Snow and the outspokenness of it. As you say, there are a lot of good lines in the lecture, which if you read at this distance you can enjoy.

But for Leavis to say of Snow, as he does at one point, *"Snow is a… well, I can't bear to bring myself to say that…Snow thinks of himself as a novelist"*, goes very far. There's a lot of disdain and a good deal of anger in Leavis' discussion. Well, that was thought to be unacceptable. He really was thought to be beyond the pale in this respect. Even some people who may have had their reservations about aspects of Snow's writing or public career thought that Leavis was going beyond the limits of acceptable discussion.

And, I think, in the initial furore—even though there were a few people who wanted to speak up for Leavis' case—the attention concentrated much more on the question of good manners, the question of the decorum of the exchange, than it did on these quite big subjects that you and I have identified here. As Leavis himself said, when he came back to comment on this several years later, nobody really addressed the central point about the shallowness of the ideals of prosperity unless they're informed by some larger idea of human flourishing.

HB: And he was quite pleased by his talk, right? Didn't he once claim that it was the greatest speech he ever made, or something like that?

SC: We can't quite tell how tongue in cheek this is because he's actually saying it to the publisher whom he's trying to persuade to publish it, so he may not be entirely straightforward about it. But he said, *"It will become a classic"*. And he said it at the time when it was being completely dumped on in this way.

It didn't become a classic, I think is the first thing to say. Throughout the 60s, apart from those who were already very well disposed to Leavis, it remained a byword for excess and personal abuse.

But I think what's happened with time—and it's very interesting how this has happened—is that Snow's reputation, if anything, has gone down. It's not so unusual a thing to happen to people after their death when they go out of the public eye and so on. But I think also the level at which Snow was writing has become clearer: it doesn't stand up all that well over time.

By the same mechanism, if you like, a few readers—I wouldn't say this is a large number yet, but a few readers—have come to see in Leavis' critique an interesting example of the tactics that might need to be involved if you're really going to take issue with a big public figure who has a lot of almost unreflective public support behind him. You're going to have to do something that will jolt people out of their comfort and which will, in some way, call attention to the mechanism that put this person there in the first place.

So as an exercise in cultural criticism, as a piece of deliberately provocative writing, Leavis' lecture is being reassessed a little now. And the qualities of his prose, which still make it difficult sometimes to read, are, I think, coming to be seen better in the way you described a moment ago: as a necessary set of weapons, in some ways, to launch this sort of guerrilla warfare that he wants to wage.

He's going to be in a minority. He's not going to be, in some sense, the one with what look like society's big guns at his command. But actually, by this series of attacks and detonations and, as mentioned earlier, taking away the podium, that big public position will start to crumble. And I think people have become more interested in that.

Questions for Discussion:

1. Whose message—Leavis' or Snow's—do you think is more relevant to the needs of contemporary society?

2. Who would you select as the modern equivalent of C.P. Snow and/or F.R. Leavis?

VIII. Lessons Learned?

Examining Leavis' impact

HB: As we look back over time and it becomes clearer what this debate was actually all about—maybe "debate" is the wrong word, in fact, more like salvos fired from passing boats—it's revealing to me to examine the context.

And I think to myself, Isn't this interesting? Here we are back in 1962, and here is somebody who was making acerbic comments on celebrity culture. Here is somebody who is talking about the value of rigorous sceptical inquiry and the belief that we shouldn't necessarily be exclusively and wholeheartedly concerned with economic prosperity without looking at the wider picture.

That wasn't my understanding of what people were thinking about or worried about in 1962. And, if anything, it seems as if the situation, from Leavis' perspective, has only become dramatically worse.

That is, some of the things that he seemed most concerned about, the notion of unflinchingly accepting an authority figure without any objective critical assessment whatsoever, are certainly worse today in an age where everybody is hyping themselves as an authority figure and wilfully, unflinchingly promoting themselves and their views at every conceivable opportunity.

So nowadays it seems to me that many of these societal issues have only become more pressing: whether or not we should look at success strictly through the filter of economic prosperity, what the role of a university should be, how one should critically train young minds and so forth.

Now enter Stefan Collini, who, from my relatively enlightened perspective now as the book purchaser—

SC: Now you've gone home and read it.

HB: Well, that helped.

And I think to myself, My gosh! There are some very strong similarities between these points that F.R. Leavis is making and these points that one Stefan Collini is making in *What Are Universities For?*

Do you regard yourself as following in the footsteps of Leavis in some of these themes?

SC: Ooh. Well, you touch on lots of things there.

HB: Yes, I apologize. I tend to do that. I have a problem asking short questions.

SC: That's fine. They're all things that, as you know, exercise me. So let me come back at the end to your final question about me, and try to start from the beginning.

I think, first of all, you're right that Leavis was diagnosing something we now call the "mechanics of celebrity culture'" although I don't think they called it that in 1962. It wasn't just in his attack on Snow. It's quite interesting. From our perspective, we think of Leavis, if we think of him at all now, as having fulfilled the role of what is now called the public intellectual: he was an academic but he gets on the public stage and in certain ways attracts wider attention and debates these issues.

He was, himself, very sceptical of that role. He saw people, his own contemporaries, doing this—appearing on the radio or writing columns in the Sunday papers or whatever it might be—and he thought that, by and large, insofar as they succeeded in becoming fairly well known, becoming celebrities, it was because they gave society what it wanted to hear. They rather sold out the standards of their rigorous, intellectual inquiry, which should have been their primary task.

In an interesting way he is not a sheltered academic in the traditional sense. As I said at the very beginning, he's not a scholar in that way in which we usually think of a scholar: patiently accumulating a lot of detail about a rather recondite subject and then very impersonally helping the advance of knowledge another small step or two by publication. His own sense of the role of the literary critic was already something much more engaged and more personal than that, and he brings that to his treatment of public themes. Again, it's this very impassioned address and something that's thought to be of very direct relevance to our lives: it's not at all removed.

And yet—and this is why he's such an interesting and complicated figure, I think—he's not trying to assume the stage as a public intellectual of the traditional sort. He doesn't think that's the way to go.

He wants, in some ways, to reserve his independence. He wants, if anything, to slightly cultivate the position of "outsiderness", or being rather underattended to, while addressing the big public realm.

It's a very tricky voice to maintain, I think. Of course, some of his critics would say that he actually wanted more public attention than he was ever willing to allow, and that's a possible reading. But I think it's nonetheless true that he not only diagnosed an early form of celebrity culture, but that he shied away from it to some extent himself. I think that's true.

The other big theme that you touched on is that nowadays, even more than in 1962, we're more exercised about the question of how far "economic prosperity as the goal" can adequately encompass things that societies ought to be aiming at.

Again, I would say that here we must not exaggerate Leavis' uniqueness or singularity. In this respect I would put him in quite a long tradition of social critics who have engaged with this, going all the way back to the figures he quotes from the 19th century, people like Ruskin and so on, who raised many of these questions.

Different moment, different circumstances, but in some ways the same kind of question: *Doesn't the driving impetus of an industrial society lead us to neglect non-economic values in some way?* That sort of question. Leavis is encouraging us to think about those sorts of questions, but I don't think that he is particularly alone in doing that, even from the perspective of the 1960s.

But I do think that he does it with a particular verbal and rhetorical force that is worth going back to. There are things about Leavis' views in general that I wouldn't endorse. I think he's much more conservative than he needs to be. He's rather horrified by some aspects of the contemporary world: changes in mores that you or I might think of as desirable and certainly harmless he's rather censorious about.

There's a puritan strain in Leavis that I certainly wouldn't share—and, as we've said already, certainly a very bellicose strain in him. But I think in his concern with the means of making criticism effective he's still very interesting reading for us. And in that sense I hope people will return to thinking about his use of the tactics of criticism.

Then we come back to the twist in the tail of your question: do I think that I'm trying to do something similar myself? Not really, I think. One of the many reasons I don't think so is that the way Leavis positions himself depends very much on some sort of "us and them" divide. There's this small, beleaguered minority of true seers, and then there's the great mass of the deluded or the benighted, who is taken in by the official or the dominant discourse.

That seems to me a very unhelpful way to think about a complicated society of the kind we live in or that he lived in. There are many more plural voices than that, surely. And one risk of that position, that rhetorical position, is of being a bit condescending to most people: as though they are rather easily duped, when quite often people don't always believe everything they see on television or read in the newspapers and have their own means of reflecting on these things.

They certainly don't need to be stirred by Leavis, or still less by me. So I don't take to his rather Manichean division into the small forces of light and the large forces of dark.

I also think he had a pretty conservative view of what might be taught in the university. Again, he stuck very much with the traditional subjects. Since the early 1960s, universities—this is true not only for Britain and the United States but for most of the universities in developed societies around the world—have expanded their range a lot. A great deal more of the cultural, social and intellectual concerns of our time now are in some sense addressed and negotiated in universities. Maybe for better or worse, but they are. Universities have become more important, but also more encompassing. And that seems to me not something that we should pooh-pooh or resist.

Leavis was very—well, he was more than cautious—I would say **hostile** to that whole expansion. He thought of universities as having a rather purer mission, I think, and probably confined to a smaller number of people.

And then within English itself, his discipline, although in some respects he was a terrific evangelist for English literature as a subject, he very much encouraged the study of "the great texts".

For him it was a rather unproblematic question of how they are the great texts or why they've become the great texts, but there are these great works of literature and we should never confuse the second or third-rate with the first-rate, and by and large we should study the first-rate. And that made him, in some respects, intolerant or at least under-appreciative of a range of other types of writing, sometimes of lighter genres, sometimes of more satirical or playful writing—

HB:—and presumably also towards the contemporary literature of his day. It's very difficult to assume that the guy down the street is in the canon, as it were.

SC: Exactly. When Leavis was a young critic, the two figures he most championed were still alive and writing: T.S. Eliot and D.H. Lawrence. Famously, as Leavis' career went on, they became the last figures he thought were of any consequence, and in fact he became more and more critical of T.S. Eliot. So as you rightly say, nobody, then, in the next few decades really measures up.

Well, again, that's a kind of conservatism or restriction of perspective that we're familiar with in critics and scholars, but it's not one I believe we should encourage. I would say that the contemporary literary world is hugely expanded since Leavis' time, partly because the anglophone world of literature has expanded so much: there's so much good writing going on in so many countries outside of Britain that use the English language, and the study of these works in universities is to be welcomed: it enriches the story.

There are all kinds of ways in which Leavis now looks to us to have some tastes and to take up some positions which really just don't speak to us, and which I wouldn't encourage.

But fundamentally, that attempt to use delicate and complex prose, which he'd honed in writing about things within universities and for a more specialized audience, to a public debate to help provoke more reflection and questioning in society about some of its received platitudes, that task—which I think he was in an angular, and awkward and not always easy way, good at—I think that's something about him which I still very much respect.

Question for Discussion:

1. In what ways is the unexpected success of Thomas Piketty's book **Capital in the Twenty-First Century** *relevant to the themes in this chapter?*

IX. What Are Universities For?
Appreciating unique strengths

HB: Well, this is my point, really, about the similarity in basic approaches between yourself and Leavis, notwithstanding the many differences. If one looks at *What Are Universities For?* and the way in which you try to engage a broader public—how you try to be provocative, your use of and examination of the role of language—my sense is that you're trying to draw attention to societally relevant questions that you feel need proper reflection and a legitimate critical faculty as we find ourselves swimming in these clichés.

Let me give you some examples that came to my mind that were Leavis-like in structure, orientation, or substance, while not necessarily in style.

When you ask these questions of what universities are for and how they are measured, their evaluation, you do a few things. There's this section of the book where you talk about the business model or the business analogy.

And there are two separate paragraphs. You first describe your job as a university professor in "business-speak", before then describing what you actually do.

Again, this is not done in nearly as bellicose or glitteringly vitriolic a way as F.R. Leavis might have done it. You're certainly not attacking the head of IBM or whatever in a personal way. But you take issue with these pat, trite phrases that are being thrown around: *"Universities should be more like businesses and this is why", "They should be more efficient and this is why".*

You draw attention to the questions of, *Well, what does it mean to be efficient at a university? How should we measure these things?*

What do these numbers actually mean? Where do they come from? How can we apply them?

You critically examine these ridiculously banal stereotypes, like, *Well, there are all these old fogies that are stuck in their ivory tower and they're trying to suck on the public teat as much as possible.* Not only do you point out that this, for the most part, is a false depiction of what's going on, but then you say, *Let's actually look at how we can carefully make these measurements, let's try to get a sense of what's actually going on.*

Another cliché that I've personally found very frustrating, is when non-academics examine the academic world and they invoke this notion of competition, this sense that there's some sort of Champion's League out there. As if, first of all, there's a fixed amount of talent in the world. As if it is not to all of our benefit to have a wonderful university in Shanghai or in North Carolina, as if that would somehow detract from the greater pool of talent of other people elsewhere. This is very simplistic in many ways. Which is not to say that the people that are making these claims are necessarily simplistic—they might be very sophisticated and those claims might well apply to their own particular realm. But they shouldn't unthinkingly transport them and unthinkingly react in a clichéd and trite manner.

So that's the sense that I had in reading your book. It's not as if you're giving concrete prescriptions—it's hardly a white paper or anything like that—it's more of an intellectual provocation so that people can think more deeply and recognize when they, in fact, have been invoking these tired ,old clichés that they should disregard.

SC: Can I take you with me wherever I go?

HB: But do you get a sense that what you are trying to do, what you are engaged in—albeit it not necessarily in the same way—is the sort of large-scale critical endeavour of which Leavis is a prime example? Would that be a good way to say it?

SC: Well, this is a delicate topic. I think one of the things that exercises me about this is that universities are, and have to be and should be, answerable to the public of their societies. I don't take the view that they have some God-given right to exist and should be given public money or private money and just left to get on with it. There is clearly a social interest lodged in universities and some account must be given of what the function universities perform is and, to some extent, how well they're doing it.

I think what has tended to happen in the last few decades is that the only language which politicians and administrators and public figures feel will have undisputed acceptance from the public at large is the language of contributing to economic growth. There are various other things that might traditionally have been said about universities, but those are in various ways contentious, or not very popular, or dismissed as subjective values, or the values of an old elite, or whatever.

The thing is not looked at very closely, but there is a strong sense among the policy-making, administrative and media classes that the only thing that's really going to justify public support in whatever form for universities, justify the whole *project* of universities (and universities on a large scale, which our societies now all have: the fact that they've expanded so much in number and in the range of their activities makes the question more central and more politically pressing), the only thing that will do that is economic growth.

I think the result of that is—and this is where we come to the very eloquent summary you gave of what I had hoped to try and argue—the result of that is that there has been a transposition of some very low-grade measures from the world of business, commerce and finance to these other cultural and intellectual worlds: *We've got to find some way of measuring output—as if it were the same sort of thing—because what we're doing is what business schools have told administrators for the last generation or two has got to be done to every organization: you've got to see how you can reduce costs and increase productivity, you've got to stop people getting stuck in outdated ways of proceeding, you've got to see if you can't bring in new ideas and get rid of old personnel. In short, you've got to run it like a very sharp-fanged business.*

And in all that, I think, what we get, as you said, are these unexamined assumptions imported wholesale from not even really the active business world—they're not what some of the best businessmen and top financiers would actually say about their own activities—but a kind of second-hand reporting of, and perception of, what is business-like about business. We get those clichés and categories imported into the judging and assessing of universities in ways that don't capture what universities are so good at.

And one of the great risks of this is that in the name of making universities more useful to society we risk damaging the ways which, in the long term, universities are so valuable to society. And it's trying to prompt us to put into circulation a language and a set of assumptions that comes a bit closer to capturing what universities really do and what they are really good at that stirs me to write this.

Now, I don't think I've done it all that successfully, and I'm not sure anyone can. It's very difficult to capture the characteristics of that kind of open-ended pursuit of inquiry because it spills over. It is in fact very disciplined, but it looks as though it slightly wanders: you can't always tell in advance what the next big or interesting questions are going to be, you're going to have to allow the people who do it a good deal of leeway to judge for themselves. The more you try to prescribe in advance what they must do, the less likely they are to make the kind of new discoveries or come up with the new perspectives which are going to be, in the end, what you really want from them.

It's a very tricky relationship. You can't give a very exact account—you certainly can't give a quantitative account—of what it is that intellectual work does at its best; and you're going to have to give the people who do it a certain amount of space in which to get on with it, while, at the same time, asserting this general sense of accountability, this general sense of social ownership of the work of universities.

At the moment, I think, things are very much tipped towards the accountability side. We're rather desperately trying to find some language and categories so that politicians and others can stand up and confidently declare, *"We've got the 18th best university in the world and productivity last year rose by 11%"* and everyone is persuaded by that.

It's gone too far in that direction. And in a way, I want us to question that a bit and see if we can't make space for some of the other ways of talking about the independent quality of good thinking and—because the two are inseparable at the end—good teaching, of making thinking happen in others in some way, which is such an indirect and chancy business; to find language which is going to make it more possible for that to maintain itself in the public realm.

That's what I hope to contribute to.

Questions for Discussion:

1. What, if anything, can universities learn from the business world?

2. What, if anything, can the business world learn from universities?

X. Constructive Engagement
Critical inquiry and watching one's language

HB: And for me as a reader, this seems structurally very similar to what you were saying earlier about Leavis, which is why I keep making this comparison.

SC: I'm sure you're going to make me into Leavis before we finish.

HB: Well, we all have our missions.

But as you commented before, it wasn't as if Leavis said, when responding to Snow, that we should ignore economic criteria. It wasn't as if he was saying, *"Technology is pernicious, it's a horrible thing, we shouldn't teach science, we should instead spend all of our days reading D.H. Lawrence".* He wasn't saying any of that at all. He wasn't denying the importance of harnessing the fruits of the scientific world, he wasn't denying the enormous impact that technology has given us all and led to better lives and so forth. He was merely saying that that's an integral part of the picture, but it's not the **only** criterion by which we should make these sorts of judgments, and it's not the only focus that we should necessarily have.

Similarly, when you're looking at the role of a university, some of your critics are portraying you as saying: *"Collini thinks that the taps should flow in an unlimited way and there should be no accountability."* You're not suggesting that there should be no public accountability whatsoever: you're very well aware of the importance of recognizing the value in some broad sense of what universities are giving to society, you recognize the importance of the utilitarian aspect of it, we shouldn't all be studying classical literature. There's simply an urging to ensure that we don't lazily slap on these tired, old clichés. That's one aspect of the picture, but let's look deeper than that.

And that's what I mean by the structural similarity between the two approaches.

SC: Yes, well, of course, your account is music to my ears because I think that's right. And as you imply, there have been some initial respondents or reviewers of my book who, for whatever reason, have decided that I'm saying, Universities are all that matters, or, universities are a world unto themselves, universities should be given the resources they need and then tell society to get lost, etc.

That seems to me to be an idiotic position to ascribe to anybody, and it's certainly not my position.

But as you say—and this is why I tried to start where I did, in working towards finding a language which can express that accountability and answerability adequately—we've got to do something more than see universities as either a glorified apprenticeship scheme in which we train people for particular, specified jobs in industry, or as some kind of industrial lab in which we come up with inventions that will make products that can be sold or cure some disease.

Those are good things to do, of course. And I say very clearly in the book that those are things, in appropriate form for their time, which universities have always done in some way, they've always had these practical purposes.

But if we *only* think those are the two kinds of things worth doing, those two aspects of an economic contribution: *just* training a kind of apprentice workforce or just applying technology towards producing industrial products, then we don't really need universities.

Universities are there to do a more complicated range of things than that. Those are very narrow functions, which they will take care of to some extent, but they won't take care of them as well unless they're also free to do their larger project of intellectual open-ended inquiry.

That's the thing that seems to me very hard to communicate in public debate. Rather than saying that universities have no responsibility to society or universities don't contribute to the benefit of society, I want to say that *unless* we allow them the freedom to do what they're really good at we will *lose* the benefit to society that they give.

And I do try a variety of tactics to attack the language about that. One that you may remember is that I have a little riff on the use of the idea of "the real world". When critics weigh in, they quite often say, *"Oh, that's all very well, but it's a little airy-fairy. In the real world, at the end of the day, it's what's on the bottom line that matters",* and they go off and develop that. That picture of the so-called "real world" is ***itself*** a fiction: it's a world in which there are these robots who pursue profit and do nothing else—and then they presumably keel over and die, although as I say in the book, their picture of the world never mentions them dying, because then they'd start to worry about all the things we worry about in universities: about the meaning of life, the aesthetic experience and all the other things.

It's important to challenge those sorts of clichés that we encounter so often now that we almost don't hear them. So we do what we can to make ourselves hear them; and make ourselves hear, therefore, that they have a point, but that they also have a limitation.

It's something that exercises me, as I say. I don't believe I've solved the problem or got it right entirely, but part of the impulse to do the book was to try to draw attention to those ways in which so much of the discourse about universities now has almost by second nature, almost by inadvertence, absorbed this sort of language and so narrowed the sphere of debate about them so much, and how damaging that can be.

HB: You said that it was difficult for people to appreciate this. Why do you think that is?

SC: I think one element that comes into this—and other people would have to say whether they recognize this in their own societies, but I think it's familiar in Britain—is that somebody who is writing about universities, who is (as it says on the book) a professor at Cambridge, who is claiming that there are inadequate aspects to the current treatment of universities and the current language about universities, is assumed, almost by virtue of that postal address, to be some privileged complainer who just wants to be left with the assumed easy and well-padded life that academics are supposed to have—although anybody who's been in a university these days would quickly see that that's not the whole story—and that he shouldn't complain. I think there's a bit of that reaction: the thing is prejudged even before you get going.

I think, too, that the attempt to be a bit playful in one's language, the attempt to use a certain amount of satire or even attempted wit in dealing with other people's views and other people's expressions, is a very delicate and dangerous weapon. It can misfire. I think people are very easily offended by this and they think that the person doing it is setting himself up as in some way superior: is sneering, is condescending.

And I have to refer to this because I do think this is an element in the reaction to some of the things—none of these things are peculiar to me, not just things I've written—but to those who, when writing about these difficult matters use those sorts of registers of prose: make the thing in some sense playful rather than simply a matter of propositional argument.

Try various ways to vary the tone of public debate and I think we're inevitably playing with fire. There are those who find that really upsetting and think that it signifies a kind of snobbish aloofness on the part of the writer.

Some of these people would be in responsible positions—running universities and their associated funding bodies—and they have a difficult job, of course. They've got all those political pressures on them to make the university or institution work and so on, and I think for some of them to be standing as far back as I'm standing and to be focusing on language and assumptions in the same way I'm doing, can come across as a bit irresponsible. It's a bit of luxury; and this is, again, why I come back to this note of being a little bit mocking.

As you know, several pieces in that book examine, shall we politely say, the language of public reports and government documents about universities and cannot help but pull some of that language apart. I think that activity is, by those who feel themselves to be in the trenches and bearing the heat and burden of the day, thought to be a bit self-indulgent. I think that's part of the element of feeling, *"this is not the 'real world'".*

Questions for Discussion:

1. Did playful use of language in public debate used to be more accepted and less incendiary than it is now? If so, what has changed?

2. How do you think the role of universities in our society will change 50 years from now?

XI. The Humanities vs. The Sciences
Ruminations on progress

HB: Let me touch on something that you mentioned in *What Are Universities For?* when you give a sense of what research in the humanities is like.

I think there are many people of a scientific persuasion who might argue something like: *"The thing about science is that it makes progress. We come up with a decision: we recognize whether the earth goes around the sun or the sun goes around the earth. We struggle for centuries about this, but we eventually get it right and then we move on and we do other things. We build this foundation that enables progress, while these guys in the humanities are just sitting there arguing the same things century after century, millennia after millennia. These problems will never be solved, there's no real sense of progress."*

This gets back to what we were referring to earlier when discussing Snow's *The Two Cultures*: this notion of the superiority of the sciences. At the end of the day, a scientist might say, we're actually making progress. We know what we're doing, we're moving towards some kind of goal, whereas these humanity guys are still arguing the same sorts things. They're still arguing about Plato, but no physicist today would invoke Aristotle.

You provide an interesting perspective here, I think, which is quite illustrative and very useful for somebody who is sufficiently open-minded to look at what people do in the humanities. You say that one of the things that people in the humanities do is worry.

Perhaps you can talk a little bit about that because I think this touches on this larger theme that we were discussing right at the beginning: this almost stereotypical *Two Cultures* notion of the different ways of thinking between the sciences and the humanities.

SC: Well, the first thing I would say, and as you know I say it in the book, is that we should recognize the ways in which we're broadly grouping together the sciences and the humanities.

The disciplines in the sciences and the disciplines in the humanities are actually doing many more similar things in a lot of their work than the stereotypical representation of them would suggest.

A great deal of the work of a scholar in most of the humanities fields is finding the evidence, testing the evidence, drawing up quite specific conclusions based on the evidence. Exactness, precision and clarity: all these values are the same, mutatis mutandis, in the different fields of the sciences and the humanities.

I think that's important because, apart from anything else, in all kinds of ways the humanities disciplines make lots of progress. All kinds of things are discovered, newly verified and tested that were not true ten years ago, and certainly not 50 or 100 years ago. Our knowledge of all kinds of aspects of history, culture, literature and so on has expanded enormously and has become, in all kinds of ways, more reliable.

So that's the first thing we ought to say: let's not exaggerate the contrast, even in method and the standing of their findings.

But then, as you know, I think the main avenue to approach this that's helpful is to realize that what we're talking about here is the expansion and deepening of *understanding*, not just the accumulation of *knowledge*.

I think this is not quite the same thing. The language of understanding is more useful to us and more relevant to what we actually do because, after all, understanding emphasizes that it has something to do with the relation of an *understander* to whatever it is that's being focused on.

The trouble with talking about knowledge is that it can make it seem like an impersonal product: once you've got it straight, you throw it on the pile and then anyone can come and take it off again and use it, or not, and you go off and find another piece.

The emphasis on the understander, I think, partly brings home to us how important it is to repossess our understanding in each generation. Not only in order to stop it dying out, but also we've got to make it intelligible to us in terms that we live in *our* time, and that's a lot of what work in the humanities is doing.

Changes in society, changes in our world, prompt us, as humanities scholars, to adopt new perspectives on things, which a previous generation thought were settled, or to put new questions to things that really just didn't occur then.

In that way there's a kind of advance—because we expand the range of the questions, we articulate the answers in ways that feed into our concerns more—but it also doesn't look like a linear advance because our questions were different from those of previous generations, and in some sense that has to be so.

In the book I give one of the most obvious examples of how a whole set of questions is opened up by changes in society that reshape fields in the humanities: the way in which the issue of gender has brought forth a range of questions about human history, human writing, human expression and human experience, which were not attended to at all adequately before.

I'm not saying that we've adequately done it in our own time—I'm not triumphalist about this—but we've started to notice some things that were not previously noticed well enough. That's affected a lot of these disciplines. English literature has a range of books to write about, and questions to put to those books, which were almost unthinkable 30 or 40 years ago.

So I think there is a kind of advance, and there are changes, it just doesn't look like the model of advance in the sciences.

Although I would just open a small parenthesis here and say that many scientists and philosophers of science would say that the standard scientific picture doesn't apply so simply to the sciences either: it's not simply a purely cumulative picture there, but often a kind of paradigm shift in what kind of thing you're trying to relate to another kind of thing and looking at in another way. Is it disputable?

HB: Yeah. They're wrong, those guys.

SC: You belong to that school, but you would acknowledge that there's another school.

HB: There is, sure. I would politely acknowledge that they exist. And that they're wrong.

SC: OK, politely acknowledge that they're wrong, as they would about you. And so that parenthesis just says, "*Let's not reify the position of the sciences either*".

I think that way of making the picture more complex—remembering that what we're talking about here is the ways human understanding functions in human experience—means that the humanities are constantly pushing new boundaries. It's just that where the boundaries are found changes because life in each generation changes.

Questions for Discussion:

1. Do you agree with Stefan that, broadly speaking, the sciences and the humanities are doing many more similar things than most people naively assume?

2. Is it possible that advances in the humanities be applied to improve our scientific understanding as well? How might that work?

XII. General Implications
The ongoing relevance of The Two Cultures

HB: Let's return now to *The Two Cultures*. By now people should have a clear understanding of what actually transpired back in 1959–1962. They should have some sense of the context of the salvos that were being fired and the reactions that they provoked.

But as far as the general public goes, there was this debate that happened. It entered the public consciousness, loosely put, in a form that we spoke earlier about between my bookseller and myself as the purchaser. So here we are more than 50 years later. Who cares? Why should we look at this again? Are people, in fact, *going* to look at this again? Will this be some sort of a lodestone for people to refer to in reframing a debate of broader societal issues? Or is this merely a part of intellectual history, some interesting things happened in Cambridge over fifty years ago?

SC: Well, you will predict now, after our conversation, that a phrase like "merely intellectual history" is going to have my critical bristles rising a little bit, because it seems to me that one of the ways we think in our own time productively is by engaging with these works. If we took other examples we would surely say that people are constantly being driven to reexamine their thoughts about freedom or freedom of expression by reading Mill on liberty, or constantly being driven to think about the role of the state by reading Rousseau on the general will.

I think that in a somewhat similar way that cluster of issues that we've tried to identify in this conversation—the identity of the humanities and the sciences and their relation, these larger issues about prosperity and goals of human life, and then the issues about how to address that in critical terms—I think that people do return to this episode somewhat, and I would say that they will continue to, because in slightly stark ways the two protagonists crystallize certain positions.

That's to say that the very ways in which Snow might be thought to be a little bland, a little conventional, in what he has to say helps make him seem to be representing a very widely held view. When you get closer it doesn't quite look like that, but he has that representative function, I think, because of those qualities.

Similarly, Leavis, precisely for the things that gave so much offense—the acerbity and the extremism in some ways of his tone—help focus the thought of, *Well, how **do** we make this case, if not like that?*

That aspect of the clash is a kind of economical way for people to reencounter these issues.

I would never say that reissues of any of those books are going to be bestsellers, but Snow's *Two Cultures* material has had a very long life in a way that you wouldn't necessarily expect. Even though it's been much criticized, people have gone back to it and continually reread it.

Leavis' response, I think, is more in doubt. It seems in some ways less far-reaching perhaps, less international, and it chimes less well with a lot of the official preoccupations of our time.

Nonetheless, I am fairly optimistic that the qualities we've tried to isolate in Leavis' attack are something that, even if people don't find themselves very sympathetic to Leavis' performance of that role, they're going to have to grapple with in some form or another if they're going to take issue with this kind of bland endorsement of prosperity and the ways in which the clichés of our time become clichés, become almost second nature to us.

If we're to be alert to that, then we're going to have to seek inspiration from, if not Leavis' attack itself, writing like that.

In the long run, having Leavis' attack brought back to our attention and having some of the characteristics of it focused on, is going to be helpful in encouraging people to do that.

So I think there'll be some life in it yet.

HB: Thanks very much, Stefan. It was wonderful to talk to you.

SC: Thank you. I enjoyed that.

Questions for Discussion:

1. Has this conversation motivated you to buy a copy of Snow's The Two Cultures lecture or Leavis' response to it?

2. Can you provide an example of a contemporary social and cultural debate that you think people will be discussing 50 years hence?

Continuing the Conversation

Readers interested in getting a deeper understanding of this topic are naturally referred to the Canto Classics editions of *The Two Cultures* and *Two Cultures?* by CP Snow and FR Leavis respectively, both of which feature a comprehensive introduction by Stefan.

More generally, readers are directed to Stefan's many books, including *The Nostalgic Imagination: History in English Criticism*, *Common Writing: Essays on Literary Culture and Public Debate*, *Speaking of Universities* and *What Are Universities For?*

Deconstructing Genius

A conversation with Darrin McMahon

Introduction
Something to Declare

In what is unquestionably the most memorable line ever uttered to a customs official, Oscar Wilde famously claimed, upon arriving in New York in 1882, *"I have nothing to declare but my genius."*

Literary scholars are quick to point out that the evidence for Wilde actually having uttered this celebrated phrase is disappointingly thin, but there's little doubt that it's the sort of thing that he very well might have said. Years later, for example, we have considerably more certainty that he confided to his friend André Gide, that: *"I've put all my genius into my life; I've only put my talent into my works."*

So whether or not Wilde actually overwhelmed American border officials with his wit is almost beside the point: a notorious self-promoter, he clearly made a habit of publicly proclaiming himself a genius throughout his life. But was he?

Well, opinions naturally differ. Perhaps a more interesting question is, *What do we mean by genius, anyway*?

Shedding light on that, among related issues, is the task Darrin McMahon has set himself in his book, *Divine Fury: A History of Genius*. It is hardly a straightforward mission, but one which naturally resonates with someone who wrote a uniquely penetrating work on the history of happiness that successfully threaded together a wide range of people and ideas from classical philosophy to the modern day.

Welcome to the world of the intellectual historian.

> *"One of the reasons why it's difficult to answer a question like, 'What is it that you do?' is in part because I became an intellectual*

historian largely because I couldn't decide what I wanted to do. I loved philosophy, religious studies, literature, classics, all these different fields—and pursuing intellectual history gave me a way where I wasn't forced to choose between them: I could put all these things together. When you study a big meaty idea like genius or happiness or whatever it might be, it's going to find its way out in so many different places. Looking at the evolution of an idea like this involves going down a lot of paths and, to me, that's fun."

Intriguingly, intellectual historians like Darrin don't always start their projects with visions of elaborate, interconnected networks through time and space dancing in their heads. Sometimes, it just happens.

"I was trained as an 18th century historian and I'm naturally attracted to pivotal ideas that emerged in the 18th century. I was aware of the fact that genius becomes a cultural ideal in the 18th century—that's fairly common knowledge. I suppose on one level I thought that I was going to write a book about the emergence of the genius as a new model of the highest human type in the 18th century and keep the scope somewhat restricted.

"That's the fulcrum of the book and that's really the fulcrum of all my work, yet the more I got into it, the more I realized that I needed to go back further, much further. It seemed silly to stop the story just as it was really getting interesting."

And we're off: from Socrates' *daimon* to Augustus' paternalism, Napoleonic presumptuousness to Nazi propaganda, Romantic mythologies to genius relics, McMahon slices and dices his way through an exceptionally broad swathe of Western history to demonstrate how the cult of genius has been used, abused and often confused.

Take intelligence. That our modern conception of genius represents a type of superhuman smartness is hardly a newsflash, but what is decidedly more subtle and intriguing is how the very notion of assessing intelligence was inextricably related to the development of our contemporary social and political structures.

*"When you attack the notion of blood aristocracy, or when you dismiss the notion that tradition and the way things have always been is the arbiter of the way that things **should** be, that creates a problem: how do you divide human society? How do you distinguish "the better" from "the worse" or "the leaders" from "the followers"?*

"What happens is that intelligence often emerges as the deciding factor, or what Americans often call "merit". And that immediately raises the problems of how you define intelligence, how you measure it, and so forth."

But even more than its standard image of the acme of intelligence, to Darrin the advent of the genius figure represented nothing less than a universal human longing.

"This is really the main focus of the book: the need for human beings to marvel in awe and wonder. That very basic human need had been fulfilled for centuries by religion. All human beings had guardian saints and we believed in apostles and prophets, and there were figures in the world who stood between us ordinary mortals and whatever lies beyond us, whatever is higher than us. And those figures acted as intercessors, as intermediaries. It's very clear to me that the genius filled many of those functions.

And now? What room, if any, is there for genius in these modern, sceptical, officiously egalitarian times?

As Darrin views it, there is a paradox of sorts: our overhyped age is drowning in geniuses, yet one frizzy-haired figure reigns supreme.

"On one level genius is everywhere. I have a couple pages at the end of the book where I talk about how there's a whole self-help literature now about how, 'You too can be a genius!', 'Learn to think like Leonardo!' and so on.

"We use the word 'genius' with total abandon; we use it for football coaches, for CEOs, for good music teachers, for the person who lives down the street and has a good music collection, and so on.

"We've democratized genius so that we have geniuses everywhere. But when you do that, the single exceptional being cannot exist. When I ask people to name a genius in the postwar world other than Einstein, I almost always get a pause but then eventually they'll come up with their own personal playlist of their favourite individuals from human history. Einstein is the last iconic genius."

It ends with Einstein, then.

It could certainly be worse. And most definitely has been.

The Conversation

I. Opening Up Sightlines
The genius of intellectual history

HB: Most of the time, when I'm talking with someone, it's very easy to start off by saying, "*Let's define the thing that you're engaged in.*"

"*You're a historian—what exactly do you mean by history?*" or, "*You're a neuroscientist—what exactly does a neuroscientist do?*"

An interesting thing about your topic is that when we talk about genius, I can't start off by asking, "*Define genius for me*" because that's *exactly* what your whole book is about: we can't clarify what we're talking about here in a few short sentences because that's really the point of the entire conversation. Is that characteristic of intellectual history as a whole, do you think?

DM: That's funny—I remember an interview I had with an AP reporter after I had written this book on happiness (*Happiness: A History*) when he tried to do just that.

"*How do you define happiness?*" he demanded.

And I replied: "*Well, that's actually the interesting question. As a historian, we look at how those definitions have changed, and we can see how they have evolved over time...*"

"*No!*" he interjected, "*What is happiness to **you**?*"

And I couldn't give a simple answer, so that became the lead line for his story: **Historian who doesn't know what happiness is writes book on happiness**.

One of the reasons why it's difficult to answer a question like, *What is it that you do?* is in part because I became an intellectual historian largely because I couldn't decide what I wanted to do. I loved philosophy, religious studies, literature, classics, all these different fields—and pursuing intellectual history gave me a way where

I wasn't forced to choose between them, I could put all these things together.

When you study a big meaty idea like genius or happiness or whatever it might be, it's going to find its way out in so many different places. Looking at the evolution of an idea like this involves going down a lot of paths; and, to me, that's fun. The negative way of looking at this is that you're a dilettante, but the positive way is that you're curious about a lot of different things.

HB: Of course, it's a huge topic. I remember musing to myself years ago that somebody should write a history of genius, but in retrospect I had a very narrowly defined view because I thought I understood what genius was.

Reading your book, I was forced to look at this concept from an etymological perspective: *What did the Greeks think of this? How did the word evolve? When does the word "genius" actually appear in the Roman world and how does it differ?*

Because of the depth of this topic your book is necessarily charting the evolution of, not just the word, but the underlying concepts and sociology. I don't think this has anything to do with dilettantism—it's simply that the very nature of the subject seems to call out for that sort of treatment.

DM: To be perfectly honest, I didn't fully appreciate how many areas this topic led into when I started. I think that's a good thing, actually. If I had a sense of how much work it was going to be, I might never have written it.

You mentioned the Greeks and the etymology of the word. "Genius" is a Latin term that referred to a guardian spirit. And there's a Greek prehistory to this idea, what they called a *daimon*—the source of our modern word "demon"—that attended individuals: great eminent individuals had a more impressive *daimon* or demon.

I was aware of the etymology of "genius" but had no idea that this early history, which is essentially demonology, would enter into the main story and then continue.

I quote from Thomas Mann at the end of the book who was very interested in this relationship between genius and madness, genius and evil, the demonic, and so forth. A lot of modern thinkers in the 19th century were interested in this relationship too, but that's something I didn't see coming. Yet it was so much fun to follow up on.

HB: So what *did* you think it was going to be all about? What did you actually think it was going to be like when you started?

DM: I was trained as an 18th century historian and I'm naturally attracted to pivotal ideas that emerged in the 18th century. Happiness was one of them. Before that, in my first book (*Enemies of the Enlightenment*), I looked at the origins of conservative thought that emerge in the same period. I was aware of the fact that genius becomes a cultural ideal in the 18th century. That's fairly common knowledge. I suppose on one level I thought that I was going to write a book about the emergence of the genius as a new model of the highest human type in the 18th century and keep the scope somewhat restricted.

That's the fulcrum of the book and that's really the fulcrum of all my work, yet the more I got into it the more I realized that I needed to go back further—much further. It just seemed silly to stop the story just as it was really getting interesting.

What happens is that the 18th century creates this new heroic figure and then builds up a whole mythology around him—a genius is almost always gendered male—and a science to support that mythology. And then you get the creation of this really powerful human type that has the capacity to do all kinds of terrible things.

HB: But it seems to me that fully appreciating all of this necessitates a significant knowledge of these prior ideas. In other words, it's not just some anecdotal points of reference—"*Oh, look at what the Greeks did*", "*Look at what the Romans did*".

When you talk about the evil genius that is instantiated in somebody like Hitler—the genius who molds people as his clay, the strong leader who breaks all the rules—that seems to connect to the idea of a strong leader who represents the will of the people. And that, it seems to me at least, is directly linked to this idea of genius as a guardian spirit—which was, in turn, deliberately used by Augustus to portray himself as "the father of the Roman people".

So it's not just that these are interesting ideas: there really *is* a path that can be traced back.

DM: Yes, I think so too. In some ways it's pleasing to hear you say that because that's almost a sort of exoneration of the type of work I do.

I was interested in intellectual history at a time when to do it was slightly looked askance at. And to do the history of ideas, in the way that I'm doing it now, really *was* taboo. There was a lot of good work done in the 60s and 70s that debunked an older approach to the history of ideas. The "great torch theory": the idea that one great thinker—Plato, say,—hands the torch to Aristotle and so on down the ages. That work seemed superficial, it seemed overly idealist in the philosophical sense, and it seemed removed from reality and the lives of ordinary people. So it was cast aside as no longer interesting.

But I'm trying to recover a type of history that takes on board many of the criticisms that have been levelled at the history of ideas—good criticisms—over the last several decades and yet recaptures this sense of the *longue durée*, recaptures some of the genuine excitement of the play of ideas over the ages.

This kind of history of ideas does have the capacity to open up sightlines over the centuries that you would miss if you didn't do it in this way. That's one of the things I find redeeming about this kind of work.

HB: This topic strikes me as particularly interesting because genius is a concept that has been around for a very long time in many different incarnations and in many different cultures, languages, sociological conditions, what have you.

There is so much depth there—and you are primarily looking at it from a Western perspective; presumably, there would be additional aspects to consider if you were to broaden your scope even further.

So there's all of this, which is subtle, fascinating, and requires a tremendous amount of study and knowledge. But then, on the other hand, this is a concept that resonates with everyone. Particular interpretations may vary, but on some level this is something that everyone on the street is familiar with and has thought about to some level.

Is that something that you're keenly aware of? Do you have a sense that this is both a meaty intellectual topic and at the same time is something that's going to resonate with many people?

DM: Yes. I wrote my first book, *Enemies of the Enlightenment*, on a fairly arcane subject. It was written as a dissertation and it was an academic book. I was proud of it at the time and I still am, but frankly, it's probably of interest to several hundred people in the world and that's about it. I remember my parents scratching their heads, saying: *"You were such a bright young man. You could have been a lawyer. Why did you do this?"*

So I had an idea that I wanted my next project to also be able to resonate with a wider readership, and *Happiness: A History* worked in that way. Happiness is something that everybody thinks about—we all want to be happy. But there's also this really deep philosophical history there and it's been part of a long conversation throughout the ages.

So yes, genius struck me as that sort of subject as well. As you say, it's just inherently interesting on some level. But it's also a window into things you wouldn't expect to see in the first place. That's the hope: that it suckers you in to seeing more than you might have at the beginning.

Questions for Discussion:

1. How frequently do you think academics experience the type of encounters like Darrin's encounter with an AP reporter? Is there anything that publishers or the media can do to improve the situation?

2. To what extent do you think "intellectual history" can be distinguished from "normal history"?

II. The Equality Paradox
Some more equal than others?

HB: Returning to what you described as your "fulcrum point", this 18th-century idea of genius, you stress two important aspects.

You talk about the fact that during this time people felt increasingly removed from the divine: the notion that the intermediaries who had previously played that role—the angels and the demons—were receding in the public consciousness and there was thus an opening for someone or something to fill that gap.

And you also discuss another important aspect of the development of genius: the concept of equality. Hopefully you'll talk more about the details, but what I'm curious about right now is: did you have these ideas going in? Did you think, as you began this project, *This is how I'm going to build my project outwards*? Or did the full extent of the impact of these factors only occur to you as you were writing the book?

DM: The religious associations that go along with genius that I make an effort to draw out, they're there and you don't have to look too closely at the phenomenon of genius to see those religious overtones.

There was a German psychiatrist, sociologist and student of genius in the early 20th century named Wilhelm Lange-Eichbaum who wrote a book, *The Problem of Genius*, which I quote in one of my epigraphs. He has a line in that book—he's writing in the 1930s—that says: *"Genius never loses its religious sub-flavour"*. And pretty early into writing *Divine Fury*, I was picking up on that idea. It's also an interest of mine; both *Happiness: A History* and *Enemies of the Enlightenment* deal with the problem of religion in a modern setting and how it finds its way into different things. So perhaps I was primed to see that, and it's pretty clear that it's there.

The issue of equality, by contrast, was something that effectively snuck up on me, because it's a real paradox. The cult of the figure of the genius as the ultimate human exception, the genius as the outlier par excellence—be it Newton, Goethe, or Napoleon—emerges at almost the same time in human history as the notion of human equality.

Of course, it takes a long time to get to real equality, and we're far from being there; yet in the 18th century, for the very first time, someone like Jefferson can say—even if it is in contradiction with his own actions—that the idea that all human beings are created equal is a self-evident truth. People were saying these sorts of things at that time. Yet genius is totally in contradiction to that.

So this interesting dialectic emerges towards the end of the 17th century between the notion of a genius figure and Western society's need for a figure like that, and this emerging notion of equality. The two are in tension from that period forward.

HB: There's also, of course, a deep tie-in between this idea of equality and class structure, certain individuals wanting to perpetuate their supremacy in some way.

DM: There's certainly that; and there's also a sociological problem that emerges when you start getting rid of the forms of hierarchy that have always divided up human beings.

When you attack the notion of blood aristocracy, as people do in the 18th century, or when you dismiss the notion that tradition and the way things have always been is the arbiter of the way that things should be, that creates a problem: how do you divide human society? How do you establish "the better" from "the worse" or "the leaders" from "the followers"?

What happens is that intelligence emerges, in some ways, as the deciding factor, or what Americans often call "merit". And that's fine on some level but it immediately raises the problems of how you define intelligence, how you measure it, and so forth.

Genius is naturally bound up in this problem. If the genius is, in a sense, the highest form of humanity then the genius might have the prospect or the license to rule over others. Napoleon is somebody who really instrumentalizes that idea.

In the 18th century you get this cult of the genius figure but it tends not to be a politicized cult.

Think of Newton. You referenced earlier this idea of the receding of the divine in the 18th century. The divine doesn't go away in the 18th century—most people aren't atheists—but I think there's quite a palpable sense that God and God's intermediaries—angels and saints and so forth—have receded and these demonic beings, in particular, might not even be there anymore. It's in that space that someone like a Newton can stand and play something like the role of the patron saint or the higher human being. Newton—at least this is the cult around him—is held as someone who can see into the very fabric of the universe and maybe even into our souls, someone who has privileged access to a higher dimension.

So you get the emergence of these kinds of figures but, as I say, they're not really politicized. Part of the genius of Napoleon is not only that he's quick on his feet, but that he uses this cult very self-consciously—and this is something that I think historians haven't fully appreciated—to create the aura around him.

Napoleon is a minor aristocrat: he doesn't have any legitimacy in terms of bloodline to be Emperor of France. Does he have a democratic mandate? Well, not really, but that's a complicated question. Nonetheless, it's not like he can completely rest on that. So how does he ground his authority and make his claim legitimate?

Well, he's a genius.

And he cultivates that image after a century that has proclaimed the genius as the highest human type. He uses this in his propaganda, in his speeches. He has priests giving Sunday sermons and addressing him as *le génie*, the genius. It creates this aura around him which is very, very powerful. In that respect he's really the first person to appreciate that potential. And that is something that Hitler will pick up on, again very self-consciously, in the 20th century and use in a terrible way.

HB: There's a self-reinforcing loop here: you're using propaganda to say that you are a genius in order to justify your rule, and then you become a "genius of using propaganda", which has also become a part of your genius. If you look at Napoleon's genius, there's a sense that part of what makes him a genius is his ability to use the genius mythology for his own ends.

But this raises the question: how much of this is a deliberately manufactured phenomenon? Even with Newton there was a sense of that.

DM: This gets to the heart of a really interesting historiographical question. There's a spectrum of people who would say that genius is entirely a social creation, that genius is, in the jargon, "constructed". Things have been written about Beethoven, too, in this respect.

Then there are those who believe that genius is an actual thing that you can measure, identify and put your finger on. Some people have it and some people don't.

I'm sort of in-between. I think it's very difficult to pull off genius if you don't have anything. I could go into a supermarket and say, "*I'm a genius!*" And in fact I quote some of these people from the 18th century who made precisely that sort of declaration.

HB: In a supermarket?

DM: Not in a supermarket, but they do it publicly—Oscar Wilde would later do this famously, in the 19th century. So you can proclaim yourself a genius but if you don't have the goods, at the end of the day, it's hard to pull it off.

Napoleon could walk into a room full of the bluest-blooded aristocrats in Europe and heads of State and he could wow them because he had that: he had the intellect, the quickness, the capacity, the vision. He could pull it off.

Yet, there is another part to this. You mentioned Newton earlier—same thing. No one doubts Newton's intelligence. And yet what made Newton into a genius was in part his own ability, and that of those who came after him, to promote his genius; to stylize himself very self-consciously, creating busts and images of him that people would put in their homes almost like religious icons, weaving a mythology around him like the story of the apple falling onto his head. These kinds of stories that once attended the saints now attend the geniuses. That's often self-conscious and the better geniuses are good at that self-promotion.

Byron is another good example of somebody who knows how to use and promote his genius for different ends—to sleep with people, to buttress his reputation, and so forth.

Questions for Discussion:

1. To what extent does a "belief in equality" imply a belief in the equivalence of particular capabilities throughout a population?

2. How might the concept of "social intelligence" fit into the concepts being discussed in this chapter?

3. If enough people are convinced that someone is a genius, does that necessarily imply that, at some level, they actually are?

III. Towards The Dark Side
The genius as rule-breaker

HB: So there are those who are doing that actively and then there are those who are publicly writing or talking about what's going on. A particularly interesting example you mention in your book is Diderot and what he writes about in *Rameau's Nephew*.

DM: Diderot is a fascinating figure. He's a great Enlightenment philosopher and he's the principal editor of the *Encyclopédie*, which is sort of the Enlightenment Bible, this compilation of all that is worth knowing. Some people would say that Diderot himself is a kind of genius. He has incredible insight, he has incredible original capacity, both as a critic and as an artist himself, and he's very interested in the notion of genius. I find him particularly fascinating because one of the points that I'm trying to focus on is the way in which genius emerges as this kind of intangible, mystical power that you can't quite put your finger on, one that has some sort of divine resonance.

Diderot is, without question, an atheist. He is, without question, a materialist. We can argue over how many there really were in the 18th century—I'm of the view that genuine atheists are fewer than we think—yet he's clearly one of them. At the same time, he writes about genius in a way that he doesn't write about anything else: he talks about "the enthusiasm" of genius.

Enthusiasm is an interesting word in the 17th and 18th century. Enthusiasm is almost always used negatively to refer to people who believe that they are in a private conversation with God—such as the religious Ranters that come out of the English Civil War, for example. Enlightenment types, in particular, use "enthusiasm" as a dirty word and Diderot is no exception.

Yet when he speaks about genius, he talks about "the enthusiasm of genius", and the possession, almost, that comes over a poet in the thrall of creation—that's actually directly related to the title of my book, *Divine Fury*, which comes from Plato's notion of the mania, or in Latin the *furor divinus*, that comes over a poet or a philosopher in the grip of production.

Diderot has a kind of materialized account of that—a medicalized account almost—of what happens to the humours during this fit and so forth. Yet he still has the idea that this kind of figure has this capacity to see where no one else can see, to draw us in with charisma in a way that no one else can. He becomes a singular being.

He is also deeply interested in the association between genius and crime, genius and transgression.

HB: Right. So geniuses seem to have this force flowing within them somehow, but as you wrote, he points out the dark side. He foreshadows disasters that can come because this wonderful creative power feels unconstrained.

DM: Yes. This actually follows directly from some of the assumptions about genius that emerged in the 18th century.

One of the things that's going on in the 18th century, and continues into the 19th century, is the overthrowing of an older mimetic aesthetic, an aesthetics based upon mimesis or imitation.

Going all the way back to Aristotle there is this idea that what great artists should do is render, in its perfection, nature or human behaviour or God's creation. There are different ways of doing that: you can render it idealized or you can do a realistic portrait painting, and so forth. And that's really the default assumption of how art ought to be done.

HB: Because you can't create. It's impossible.

DM: Right. You can't create. This is the other interesting notion that I like to point out: the idea that only God can create is really deeply tied up in Western theology. God is "the creator omnium": he's created the whole world and everything in it, and all we can do is sort of reproduce God's perfection.

In the 18th century you start to get people challenging this notion of a mimetic aesthetic. They start putting forward the belief in the possibility, and also lauding the possibility, that human beings can create for themselves, create originally, that they can do something that no one else has ever done before. They can bring into being a new idea or a new image.

By the Romantic period, this is now seen by some—for Immanuel Kant, for example, the German philosopher who writes about genius at length—as a fundamental aspect of the very *definition* of genius: a genius is somebody who creates originally, who doesn't imitate, who doesn't copy. From the latter part of the 18th century forward, copying and imitating are seen as negative things; to copy something is to be second rate, to not have your own ideas.

How this ties into the idea of evil or transgression is that the genius is seen as a kind of lawmaker. The genius lays down rules in art, say, that other people follow. People who have talent might be able to follow the rules of a genius, but the talented can't have genius—genius is seen as something else.

And that moves very quickly, I think, from aesthetics to something else: the genius is *by definition* a rule-breaker. The genius *doesn't* follow the norm, the genius does something that no one else does.

HB: He sets his own rules.

DM: Exactly. And that may involve breaking rules. As you say, that link is explicitly made by Diderot in a very prescient way in his dialogue *Le neveu de Rameau* or *Rameau's Nephew*.

Interestingly, it wasn't published in Diderot's lifetime and is first published in German. Guess who does the translation? Goethe, the great German poet, who himself was deeply interested in genius and in notions of transgression, the "daemonic" as he calls it. So that's kind of an interesting link too.

Anyway, in the 19th century this connection between the genius and transgression and abnormality emerges in a very self-conscious way. By the end of the 19th century you have crime fiction, like Sherlock Holmes, with the figure of Moriarty who's the kind of evil genius, who's described as "the Napoleon of crime". He makes rules for himself and he breaks rules. All geniuses do that on some level. All geniuses destroy, on some level, in order to create.

Questions for Discussion:

1. Is there such a thing as being "wholly original"? To what extent does the act of creation always involve building upon the work of others?

2. In what ways are the "rules" or "laws" involved in the creative arts both similar and distinct from those of the natural sciences?

IV. Romantic Genius
Reinvented, suffering and zealous

HB: So from that perspective, perhaps there's a sense that if you're quietly sitting in your study producing something then perhaps that doesn't qualify you as a genius. On the other hand, there are the neglected geniuses, the forgotten geniuses…

DM: Well, exactly. "*The unacknowledged legislators of the world*", to use Shelley's great phrase: the poet can quietly change the world simply by sitting in his study and writing poetry. The Romantics are funny about this. On the one hand, they want desperately to be seen and heard and felt. But on the other hand, they invent this cult of "the undiscovered genius", the unacknowledged genius, that person who just doesn't have that lucky break.

One of the things the Romantics are very good at is going back, looking again at Western history, and finding geniuses. You mentioned before that in some ways geniuses have always existed and that's true, but at the same time it's not.

It's true in the sense that all cultures and all times have had notions of "heroes of the mind": there have been wise men, great poets and so forth. But the way the genius gets defined in the 18th century is really a modern creation. So what happens post-18th century is that people start looking at human history and ransacking the past to find geniuses.

It's in the 18th century that Shakespeare and Homer are explicitly classified as geniuses. They're described as such, with the characteristics and qualities that are a part of the modern notion of genius: original thinker, transgressive and so forth.

Shakespeare fits the part perfectly: he has no formal education yet he seems to produce all these poems and plays out of his head without any formal training. The Romantics are good at finding all kinds of geniuses, particularly in the Renaissance. That's one of the reasons why people often associate genius with the Renaissance. There are early identifications of the type in Michelangelo, Leonardo, and Raphael but they're still not geniuses in the modern sense.

HB: There was also this imprisoned poet you mentioned.

DM: You're referring to Torquato Tasso, the great Renaissance poet, who goes mad and gets put into an institution—a mad house—against his will and he becomes a sort of cult hero for the Romantics. Eugène Delacroix, the great French painter, does several famous paintings of Tasso in a madhouse. In those paintings he's portrayed as a martyred saint, driven mad by an uncomprehending public. He's alone and isolated, and yet he's a higher being. He's suffering for his genius.

That's another Romantic trope that grows even stronger in the 19th century: that genius is a blessing, but also a curse. It's a curse that one has to suffer for, and the preferred curse is a kind of neurosis leading to madness, in the extreme—"moral insanity" is the term that some of the figures in the 19th century used—in other words, crime.

HB: It's also a great justification for not being sufficiently recognized in one's lifetime.

DM: Absolutely. One of the people that I write about at some length is Francis Galton, the cousin of Charles Darwin. He was one of the first scientists to study genius formally and to try to figure out how many geniuses would emerge from a given gene pool, even though he naturally didn't have any formal knowledge of genetics at the time.

Galton comes to the conclusion that there's no such thing as an "unacknowledged genius", because an integral aspect of genius is not only natural aptitude but also what he calls "zeal": the desire to be a genius, the desire to be eminent, joined with the capacity for hard labour to carry it out. All genius, he believes, leaves a track record that you can trace by looking at the number of times that person is cited in newspapers or the national dictionary.

HB: Very scientific.

DM: Yes. I'm very sceptical of many of these 19th century and even more modern attempts to pinpoint genius, to study it scientifically. I think there's more going on there.

HB: But it's interesting that it implicitly enfolds this notion of propagandizing and utilizing the cult of genius, to some extent. Because according to these criteria, independent of whatever has been produced, if somebody hasn't been sufficiently well recognized in his lifetime, then he doesn't qualify.

Had I gone off to an island somewhere and come up with the general theory of relativity in 1910, five years before Einstein, I still wouldn't qualify as a genius because nobody would have known about it.

DM: But on some level we *do* sort of buy into that. Take the case of Wallace and Darwin. The theory of evolution is pretty well there within Wallace's work and yet we still think of Darwin as a genius and Wallace not so much.

Questions for Discussion:

1. Can genius be successfully modelled by the small fraction of extreme cases at the outer limit of the bell curve of any population, or is it something quite different?

2. How much of our conviction of the level of genius of any creator is directly related to how influential his work currently is?

3. Does the general reluctance to attribute the label of "genius" reflect more than simply a male-dominated perspective of human achievement?

V. Nature vs. Nurture

A threat to equality?

HB: When these ideas started coming out in the 18th century I can imagine that this naturally rekindled the debate of nature versus nurture: is genius—whatever it is—something innate or can it somehow be taught? I'm guessing that there were people who lined up on both sides and the pendulum swung back and forth. Presumably, in fact, this discussion started considerably earlier.

DM: Sure. On some level you can trace the debate back all the way to the ancient world. The Romans had this idea of *ingenium*, which is your inherent talent, as opposed to what's acquired through learning and training. There was an ancient Greek debate around this too: do the best poets just have it, are they given their abilities by the Gods, or is it born into them? So yes, on one level, the debate it's very old.

What I find particularly interesting, and this is a theme that I stress in the book, is that you have this debate in the 18th century to be sure, and you hear voices that in some ways you would expect to hear. In other words, you get Enlightenment rationalists who become very sceptical of earlier notions of divine infusion or inspiration—

HB: Or enthusiasm.

DM: Enthusiasm, exactly. Inspiration comes from *inspirare*: "to be breathed into by a god", and of course there was a literal understanding of that. The Christian tradition, for a long time, had the notion that saints and angels revealed wisdom to people and that higher figures were in special traffic with the other world.

So you get people casting scepticism on this notion and applying a new epistemological view that John Locke, in a sense, crystallizes and many people tweak in the 18th century. Locke has this idea of the *tabula rasa*: that we're born into the world with a mind like a blank slate, or a blank chalkboard, and the world writes on it through experience. Who we are and what we know is a product of what we've seen and done in the world.

So people take that argument in the 18th century and they begin to say that genius is fundamentally a product of input. It's what kind of experiences you have, what kind of exposure you get—the earlier the better—so on and so forth. It leaves open the prospect that you could almost *make* a genius if you engineered the perfect mind.

I think there's a lot to be said for that way of looking at this and there are modern proponents of that view. You've probably heard of the 10,000-hour rule that was invented by my psychologist colleague Anders Ericsson and Malcolm Gladwell made explicit mention of. This is the idea that you have to have 10,000 hours of training in order to be good at anything.

HB: *But then anyone could do it*, goes the argument.

DM: Well, maybe. But if you look at Mozart, he had a father who was a music teacher and so he got all this early exposure and that explains Mozart.

HB: By 3? Did he have 10,000 hours by the time he was 3?

DM: Well, that's the thing, right? Of course it gets tricky. But there are people who defend that line of argument, and I think it's quite compelling on many levels.

What's interesting about the 18th century, and somewhat surprising, is that this argument loses out by and large. Yes, there are still people who are around in the 19th and 20th centuries who put the emphasis on nurture as opposed to nature, but the way genius gets defined in the 18th century is precisely that it *can't* be learned; genius *cannot* be acquired.

There's always this invidious distinction between talent and genius. You can learn how to be a talented piano player: you get lessons, you practice, and so forth but you can't learn how to be a genius. You either have it or you don't. That's the defining characteristic of original genius—and "original" here has this double sense of being unprecedented but also original: at the origin, at birth.

So in the 18th century people start to get really interested in prodigies, and this is one of the reasons why Mozart is such a fascination: he seems to be an indication of how genius should look at birth and how genius ought to just emerge naturally. Then in the 19th century you get scientists trying to precisely pinpoint, identify, locate and classify it.

But as I say, the definition of genius that wins out into the 20th century, is a play on the old Latin line, *poeta nascitur non fit*, that poets are born and not made. Similarly, genius is born and not made—you either have it or you don't. You can certainly *develop* your genius but you can't *learn* how to be a genius.

HB: During the Enlightenment, did people recognize the irony of that? These great Enlightenment thinkers believed in scientific rationality, they believed in being able to measure things. Was there anybody who said: *"Wait a minute, this whole idea smacks of being inspired by the Gods; it's mystical, enthusiastic"*? You mentioned that Diderot was able to compartmentalize things so that while sneering about religious enthusiasm he was nonetheless still able to speak about genius in similar terms. Were there people around who said: *"Hold on guys, you've missed the boat here: this sort of talk is not actually in keeping with the spirit of the times that we so strongly believe in."*

DM: I haven't tried to quantify that sentiment but I thought that voice would have been more robust. There was certainly an attempt, which began in the 18th century and continues into the 20th, to de-emphasize the quasi-religious, mystical aspects of genius and make genius into a science.

But what I think happens—and this is one of the arguments in the book—is that science somehow kind of re-enchants genius.

When Galton quantifies that genius is one in a million or one in ten million, he is ascribing these superhuman powers to this exception of nature who has the ability to do things that ordinary human beings can't. This gives the genius a sort of mystical quality and lends itself to a religious aura or awe. That's one thing that happens. There's a sort of guilty conscious: people are trying to make a science out of genius even though, in the process, they don't make it any more rational or scientific.

But there are also people—and I think this is the more interesting Enlightenment-related playing out of this idea—who were uncomfortable not only with the religious packaging of genius and the mystical aura around genius, but with the conflict between genius and the notion of equality. So you get a very vibrant debate during the French Revolution about what, literally, to do with genius. And the middle part of my book is focused on some of these stories.

During the French Revolution, they converted the great former church that Louis XV had built into what's now the Panthéon, the resting place of great men which was modelled on the Roman Pantheon. One of the first people they put in there is Voltaire, and then Rousseau, and they're having this whole discussion about who should go in there and who should not. The great French philosopher René Descartes had died in Sweden almost a century and a half earlier, and there's this vigorous debate over whether or not he should be put in the Panthéon.

One of the people who was arguing on behalf of this says that it's a "crime against genius" that he hasn't been hailed and treated like Newton was treated in Britain, being buried in Westminster Abbey and so forth. And then a further debate about this very characterization ensues—whether or not it's right to be treating our geniuses and great men like they were saints. People actually point this out.

There's a whole cult of the body associated with genius, and that's another aspect that I find really fascinating: the way bodies of geniuses are treated like relics. There is literally a trade in the skulls and bone fragments of geniuses in the 19th century to the extent that—and this is my favourite example—someone pays good money in London for what purports to be Napoleon's penis. It was bought by an American, and was owned by a urologist—of course—at Columbia University until relatively recently.

Anyway, that is an aside, because the more interesting debate is about what to do with geniuses in a society that has proclaimed equality as one of its central values. This problem isn't lost on people.

They change the calendar at the height of the French Revolution. They get rid of the Christian calendar and they date time from the beginning of the French Republic. And of course you can't have things like Saints' days and religious holidays because you've gotten rid of all of that as well. So what do you do? Well, one of the things they put in place is a "Festival of Genius": a day to honour genius. They're debating where this should go in the Revolutionary calendar and whether it should take precedence over other festivals.

Robespierre, the great Jacobin leader and radical, stands up and says: "*Caesar was a genius, but Cato the Younger, the great Republican, was a man of virtue. Virtue is more important—is better—than genius.*"

HB: And that's what we should be celebrating.

DM: Yes. So he gets the calendar rearranged so that Virtue is the first of these revolutionary festivals and Genius is afterwards.

But it also leads to a debate in the National Convention over the place of genius in a society that proclaims equality. It's a problem that really troubles Robespierre and some of the Jacobins who ask, "*Are we erecting an aristocracy of genius?*" Some of the best Enlightenment minds are aware of this problem, such as Rousseau and Condorcet, the mathematician who is also a French revolutionary.

Condorcet is precisely the sort of Enlightenment rationalist that you talked about before: he wants to improve education, to give everyone access to it with the goal of producing more Newtons than the old regimented hierarchical society could produce. Yet, if you push him—and he pushes himself—he doesn't believe that all intelligence is equal. He believes that there are certain leading lights, geniuses, as it were. So, what do you do? How do you create a culture in which these kinds of people can still emerge, and yet one in which people still have equality of access?

It's a similar problem for Rousseau. Rousseau, interestingly enough, doesn't believe in the equality of human intelligence. That's one of the reasons why he's so keen to construct a society in which virtue is a kind of levelling force that keeps people as social equals, because he fears genius. He thinks that inequality of intelligence will lead to inequality in human societies—which, of course, happens: we've built economies, very powerful ones, on the basis of that.

And we sort of pat ourselves on the back and say: *"Well, this is just how it's supposed to be, because it's in nature."* Yet it's problematic from a perspective of justice and equality.

Questions for Discussion:

1. Is the standard image of genius incompatible with hard work and long-developed expertise? To what extent does a genius have to create his masterpieces effortlessly?

2. To what extent does a belief in the innate nature of genius reflect a "fixed mindset"? (For more background on fixed and growth mindsets, see the Ideas Roadshow conversation with Carol Dweck, **Mindsets: Growing Your Brain***)*

3. Can you give examples of other occasions where the argument, "This is just how it's supposed to be, because it's in nature" fails on moral grounds?

VI. Evil Genius
The other side of the coin

HB: It's certainly possible to envision a world in which we have the best educational system, the greatest amount of social equality and justice where everyone is taught to the best of his abilities. And then, somehow, on top of that, you could imagine that true geniuses would also emerge. It seems to me that such a world is logically possible, but it never seems to happen that way—things seemed to happen in quite a different way.

And part of this, it seems to me, at least in the 19th and 20th century, is linked to this notion of the genius figure being able to break all the rules. From Diderot musing about the dark side of genius to the Romantics talking about how part and parcel of being a genius is being able to destroy the old order, there seems to me to be a pretty direct line from Napoleon right through to Hitler.

Here is this failed painter who somehow succeeds in transforming himself into a genius who arrives to destroy the oppressive old order and incarnate the will of the people. That's the Nazi propaganda, right?

DM: Very much so. This is related to what the Germans would call *Geniegedanke,* or the thinking around genius—an idea that emerges out of German Romanticism in the 19th century. The fact that a failed artist, as you say, would have cottoned on to this is not at all surprising.

What is surprising, to me at least, is the extent to which historians haven't really picked up on it, although there are naturally some exceptions.

But by and large the way in which Hitler very self-consciously presents himself as a genius and then uses that as part of his propaganda has been downplayed. You could speculate as to why that was the case; even today it's still slightly disconcerting to use the words "Hitler" and "genius" in the same sentence. Of course, I hasten to add that I'm not making any judgement on his intelligence or lack thereof; that's not what I'm interested in doing. I'm interested in examining how he uses this concept.

And he does. It's there for everyone to see. If you read *Mein Kampf* it's all spelled out there. He writes about genius at some length for several pages and he ties himself into this German belief that emerges in the 19th century, and then gets scientized and publicized, that *"the exception can speak for the whole"*. In other words, that the outlier can somehow incarnate the whole of the people.

HB: Perhaps even "***should*** speak for the whole". He hails himself as a saviour, of course.

DM: Absolutely, very much so. And this is where he uses, again quite self-consciously, the quasi-religious overtones that genius has: somebody who can speak for and be a ventriloquist for the will, a prophet figure, a figure of redemption who can heal, and so forth. And from very early on in his career he goes to great lengths to stylize himself in this way.

One of the things he does is to befriend Houston Stewart Chamberlain. Chamberlain is born in Britain and later moves to Germany. He's a German speaker and a great admirer of German culture, he marries Richard Wagner's daughter, and he's living in Wahnfried, Wagner's home in Bayreuth, which is a kind of spiritual centre of a genius cult in the 19th century.

Chamberlain wrote these long cultural histories extolling German racial and cultural superiority, and he puts a huge emphasis on the genius figure. Hitler visits him and becomes very close friends with him. Right after their first meeting, Chamberlain writes a letter to him—he's close to the end of his life at this point—and he says: "*I have faith in German culture if we can still produce men like you.*" And, of course, Hitler then uses this to ally himself to this genius cult that surrounds Wagner, who is, famously, Hitler's favourite composer.

HB: So he justifies himself. He says: *"Look, Chamberlain says I'm the coming man, I'm a saviour, I'm a genius—*

DM: *"—and I'm a part of"*, what the Germans called, *"the brotherhood of genius. I'm in that family."* And then this becomes a trope in his propaganda. Again, you can ask the question, *He has **something**, right?* He's a complete outsider to German culture, which is in many ways one of the most advanced cultures in the world, and to be able to pull off this hoodwinking, it takes a certain something.

Yet, from my perspective, the more interesting question to ask is, *How does he do it?* The way in which he builds this mystical aura around himself using the cult of genius is really fascinating.

And then, of course, when he's in power, Goebbels and his propaganda people really emphasize this to great length. Hitler goes on all these, in a sense, pilgrimage visits: to the house where Nietzsche died in Weimar, and the Weimar of Schiller and Goethe. He goes around the country and orchestrates very strategic photo-ops, associating himself with these great figures of German culture, presenting himself in this way.

HB: And you mentioned before how this ties in with his virulent and explicit anti-semitism. The Jews are portrayed as possessing this mimetic quality: *"They're clever; they can imitate, but they're not the real creators. And by being just a clever imitator, you're actually polluting the genes of the real creators, the real German people whom I, Hitler, represent as a father figure"* and so forth.

Obviously these things are morally repugnant yet it's important to study them because one gets a better understanding of the context, which, in a sense, opens our eyes. One can say: *"Ah, **this** is what he's doing. **This** is how he's actually able to achieve his goals."*

And as a complete non-expert, I wonder: is your interpretation of his conspicuous use and abuse of genius new? Is this something that other people have remarked upon as well?

DM: I think the genius cult around Hitler has been really downplayed. There have been one or two German historians who have addressed the topic. Jochen Schmidt wrote an intellectual history of genius in Germany and he talks about how Hitler uses this language.

There was a study that came out a number of years ago on Hitler's passionate interest in art collecting—all very cheesy and kitschy kinds of art—but nonetheless it illustrates how Hitler thought of himself: he saw himself as an artist. Literally to the very end of his life, in the bunker in Berlin, he's obsessing over this model to remake Linz, the city in Austria where he was from, he sees this as being his legacy. In his mind, he could have been a great architect but he channelled his genius in another way.

HB: Has this been downplayed because people are fearful that by using the word "genius" and "Hitler" in the same sentence, they would be somehow condoning his actions or elevating his stature? Is that the great fear?

DM: I think that's part of it. In the book I mention an incident a couple of years ago when Michael Jackson, the pop singer, said that Hitler was a genius about something or other—his set design, I think—and of course everyone called him an idiot and he was slammed, justifiably so. But that I think does point to how this is still an extremely sensitive subject.

Also, I think there was a real emphasis after the war to disconnect Hitler's early life, his failure as an artist, and his more "successful", as it were, life as a politician and say that the two weren't related at all. There was also a tendency to really emphasize his failure in a psycho-biographical sense: the resentment that was created by his inability to be admitted to art school, or what have you.

The historiographical trend in the last decade or so has really emphasized the way in which his early artistic interest and his later political interest go together. One author uses a nice phrase: "*Hitler pursued art by other means.*"

I believe that these things *do* go together, but I think that after the war there was an attempt to either paint Hitler as a madman or as a second-rate figure who catered to all that was low and base. I think there was also an unwillingness in German culture to somehow associate Hitler with what was thought of as the best of German culture. So you have "the good Germany" of Beethoven and Goethe, which is always invoked when you talk about genius, and you have "the bad Germany"; and to put those two together was really problematic. But I'm not at all sure. I'm really just speculating here.

HB: Of course, it's always a very sensitive subject when one tries to examine motivations behind what was unquestionably one of the most despicable regimes in human history. But what confuses me here is that there are two very different statements. One is *"This guy is a genius"*—the asinine Michael Jackson statement, if you will. But the other is: *"This guy used the cult of genius for his own horrific ends."*

They're completely different things, in my view—and of course, it's the latter that you're stressing. You're *not* saying that "he's a genius", of course. You're saying that he was very consciously, very deliberately invoking this particular notion in order to achieve his ends which were largely, objectively "politically successful" in terms of him attaining power, which was subsequently used to inflict unspeakably horrific consequences on millions of innocent people.

But why do you think people are so hesitant to examine this second claim in a rational way?

DM: I do try to explain this a little bit in the book. And one of the things that I try to show is that the association with evil gets covered over after the war.

In particular, I mention this very famous *Time* magazine cover that comes out right after the war that shows Einstein as a nice, grandfatherly-looking professor, and there's a mushroom cloud going off in the background with the equation $E = mc^2$ written into it.

Einstein had very little to do with the development of the atomic bomb. He played a small role in justifying its development to the Roosevelt administration, but that's about it. But that's a really interesting image, and it still gets at the way in which the genius, even a good genius like Einstein—who, in the mythology, contributed to saving the free world by helping to develop the bomb—is still in possession of this power, this technology, that can do terrible, terrible things. Of course, there's a great suspicion around Einstein from the FBI and others: is he going to sell our secrets to the Soviets? What's going to happen?

But over time that emphasis and that association to evil and transgression really gets downplayed. That also has to do with, in part, the emergence of the scientist as the default figure of a genius in a way that wasn't really the case previously. You had Newton in the 18th century and there were a few other scientists, but by and large, the great geniuses early on tended to be poets, artists, men of letters, and not scientists.

HB: But that doesn't conform, presumably, to the Romantic tradition: this idea of making your own rules. If you're a scientist you're interpreting and figuring out what the rules are.

DM: Right, exactly. You're figuring out what is already there. We can talk at length about the way in which Newton and Einstein actually *do* enter into this discussion, and I think they give one a sense of the real creativity involved in any kind of interesting scientific enterprise.

HB: You had me at hello. They're geniuses. I'm with you on that one.

One of the things I was not sufficiently appreciative of is this almost apocalyptic battle between good and evil geniuses that you portray between Einstein and Hitler.

Obviously Hitler was going to be wildly disparaging of anyone who was Jewish and successful, and Einstein was wildly successful. Hitler made all these idiotic claims about "Jewish science" and so forth. But I hadn't fully appreciated these actions in light of Hitler's continual persistent use of the genius myth to justify his *own* aura.

So what you're really seeing, it appears, is this great battle where Hitler has erected himself as a genius, a spokesperson for the German Volk, in the tradition of the Romans—namely Augustus—while denigrating all Jewish accomplishment as only mimetic, as clever; "*They don't have their own culture; they're just copiers,*" and all this nonsense.

But then he runs into this clear, unequivocal case of somebody who has just transformed our understanding of nature at its most fundamental levels, who is the poster boy of genius in the civilized world, and what is he going to do about that? How is he going to combat this Einstein figure?

So at the end of the day, notwithstanding the best efforts of *Time* magazine, Einstein emerges triumphant, and from that point forwards genius has this intuitively positive quality associated with it. Here's this wonderfully brilliant, scientific, grandfatherly fellow and, as you put it, that's really the end: there are no more geniuses after that. It really has this ring of good and evil. Good triumphs at the end of the day and then that's it. That's the end of genius history.

DM: Well, my history is sounding uncomfortably like a screenplay, but I think that there *is* a dramatic quality to this. And I think this is very much a part of Nazi consciousness.

The Jewish genius is a problem. And it's not just a problem for the Nazis, it becomes a problem for Galton. When Galton starts quantifying things, he says: *"You look at the Jews and they're disproportionately producing people of high intelligence and eminence."*

Lewis Terman, the American psychologist who instrumentalized the IQ exam that was originally developed in France by Binet and Simon, he noticed the same thing in his pools. Both he and Galton have anti-semitic tendencies, so they're not comfortable with this.

Of course for the Nazis it's even more of a problem, and it's a problem that stares them in the face. The number of Jewish Nobel Prize winners is highly disproportionate to the size of the population. The presence of great Jewish scientists in the German scientific establishment in the early part of the 20th century is just overwhelming. So, what to do with this?

As you alluded to earlier, the Nazis pick up on this invidious distinction that has developed since the 18th century between genius and talent. It's a distinction, I should point out, that is still around—you occasionally hear people say discriminatory things like, for example: "*Asians are good mimetic violinists but they have no inner creativity, no soul*".

This is a deeply unsavoury, racist thing to say. And this same idea is instrumentalized by the Nazis to sort of explain away Jewish intelligence as: "*The Jews are clever but they're not geniuses*". So when Einstein emerges, it's pretty difficult for them to keep making these claims and deny his genius. They try their best of course; there are people who say, "*The theory of relativity is Jewish science*" and so forth.

In my mind—and again this is speculation—one of the reasons why Einstein really rankles is that he gives the lie to this myth that has been constructed, this myth that has real, powerful consequences. I probably don't draw enough attention to this in the book, although I allude to it.

It's very clear that Hitler's power over his generals is, in part, like Napoleon's power over his generals. He makes some rash decisions early on that don't follow the rules, that break the rules, but they have spectacular success and it gives him this power. He's kind of a madman, right? There was also this idea in the 19th century, which can be traced back to the ancients, that geniuses are slightly unstable, that they rant, that they're, if not mad, then severely neurotic.

In fact—let me just make a quick aside for a moment—there was a Jewish-Italian doctor, Cesare Lombroso, an important criminologist in the 19th century who also becomes an important student of genius. When he's talking about Jewish genius he says that one of the reasons why Jews have become so eminent is because they have a higher proportion of neurotics because genius and madness go together. It's kind of funny.

HB: I wonder what Woody Allen would make of that.

DM: Exactly.

Anyway that aspect of Hitler's persona that I was just referring to—the fact that he's ranting and wild-eyed, combined with what seem like irrational decisions that are nonetheless successful—these things actually *enhance* his appeal early on in the regime that will help him to solidify his power later on.

I think the way that he uses these moments in relation to his genius cult is very revealing.

Questions for Discussion:

1. Has the lack of will to objectively understand Hitler's rise to power made us less conscious of the mechanics of populist movements in general?

*2. Can a Hitler-like figure arise, in principle, **anywhere**? Or are there some necessary sociological conditions required in order for someone like that to be "politically successful"? If so, what might those be?*

VII. Geniuses Everywhere
The superhuman condition?

HB: Einstein, on the other hand, was, for the most part, notoriously uncomfortable with being mythologized, the idea that he was so incredibly exceptional. He did, admittedly, clearly enjoy playing to it to some degree, but, by and large, he was deeply uncomfortable with this notion that he was so completely off the scale compared to anybody else around him. He was obviously aware of the brilliance of other scientists and the brilliance of other people in whose circles he might have travelled. But he recognized the need that people had to erect this mythological genius type of figure.

I'd like you to talk a little bit more about that because that's a common strain that's running through your work: this awareness, this acknowledgment that at different points in history we, as humans, have had this need to put certain people on a pedestal. So it's not just a case of: *"Oh, that Hitler or Napoleon—how did they somehow manage to hoodwink us?"* They hoodwinked us because there was this societal need.

DM: In fact, you've reminded me of a point that I forgot before. We were talking about why it is that people haven't recognized the full extent to which the Nazis used this genius mythology, and I made the point that on the one hand it draws uncomfortable associations with the "good genius cult" in Germany around Beethoven, Goethe, and so forth. But I think it also points out what you alluded to just now: this human need to believe in higher human beings. This is, of course, very much in tension with the belief of human equality.

I think there are actual psychological reasons for this. Earlier I mentioned Anders Ericsson, my psychologist colleague who thinks about these things—we've had some interesting discussions about this. One of the things that he and I speculate is that even on the level of the family, parents have limited resources: they don't have enough time or energy to develop all their children the same way. So if they can identify one child as the gifted one, that somehow justifies them in spending an inordinate amount of time taking that child to hockey practice, or whatever it might be.

So then on a societal level, we have investments in genius that also serve functions which get us off the hook for our own inadequacies or for societal inadequacies.

If genius is something that spontaneously emerges, if even someone like Louis Armstrong, with all the hurdles that he faced, can emerge as one of the great musicians of the 20th century, we don't need to have good schools, we don't need to make better societal arrangements. So it gets us off the hook in that respect and it also justifies our own deficiencies.

But I think there's something more going on, and this is really the main focus of the book: the need for human beings to marvel in awe and wonder. That very basic human need had been fulfilled for centuries by religion. All human beings had guardian saints and we believed in apostles and prophets, and there were figures in the world who stood between us, ordinary mortals, and whatever lies beyond us, whatever is higher than us. And those figures acted as intercessors, as intermediaries. It's very clear to me that the genius fills many of those functions.

Geniuses emerge from the 18th century forward as people who are "out there", who can see into the very fabric of the universe and relay that information to us in the way that Einstein can, or who can see into our souls the way that great poets can, who can know us better than we know ourselves.

That gives us comfort, that there are people like that out in the world. Yes, that can be politicized in an unsavoury way, but in a very basic way I think it's just sweet and innocent, and not necessarily dehumanizing—although it certainly does have that potential.

HB: Of course there's the obvious danger of the charismatic figure coming in but there's also the obvious danger of not willing to think for one's self; this notion of abdicating intellectual responsibility.

Surely if you're somebody who is a fervent believer in equality and general education and so forth, one of the most important things you're trying to do is—not so much educate the citizenry about point A, point B, and point C—but about *how* to think independently, and how to think critically.

You allude to this tension throughout the book. I have long been amazed at how Einstein, who as we've said so often now is **the** modern icon of genius for everyone around the world and yet virtually nobody has any real comprehension of what he actually accomplished.

That's always struck me as a little bit odd but perhaps in light of what you're saying, it's not odd at all. There's a sense that these ideas are so complicated, so impenetrable, that only a genius would be able to understand it. It's like going to a magic show: there's a willingness to be overwhelmed, mystified and to be in the presence of unintelligible excellence and so forth.

But it's interesting that nobody after Einstein has been acknowledged as a genius. One of the reasons why Einstein is still so iconic is that we can't point to anyone else from the 60s, 70s, 80s, or even into the present day.

DM: There are two things going on here. One thing that you've alluded to that's really important, which I think is part of Einstein's appeal and part of the appeal of genius, is what Einstein recognized himself and called *"the mystery of non-understanding"*. He says explicitly that part of the appeal of his genius was that people didn't have the slightest clue what he was actually doing. There was just this idea that there is someone out there who sees into the very fabric of space and time, and that's encouraging.

Genius as it emerges in the 18th century serves this function. One of the ways that I explain this is that at the very same time the world is being disenchanted, being purged of its mysterious beings, genius serves the role and performs the function of re-enchanting the world, reintroducing mystery and the sublime back into human experience. So that's one point.

This other question of whether Einstein is the last genius or whether the cult of genius dies with Einstein, on the one hand when you say that to people they immediately look at you oddly because on one level genius is everywhere. I have a couple of pages at the end of the book where I talk about how there's a whole self-help literature now about how, "*You too can be a genius!*" and "*Learn to think like Leonardo!*" and so on.

We use the word "genius" with total abandon; so much so that Marjorie Garber, a literary critic at Harvard, in *The Atlantic*, wrote this wonderful article called "*Our Genius Problem*", in which she says that we simply use the word too much. We use it for football coaches, for CEOs, for good music teachers, for the person who lives down the street and has a good music collection and so on.

In some ways this "democratization of genius" is a working out of this long tension with equality and a way of robbing the single individual of this power which is potentially dangerous. So on the one hand this is a good development that we have "democratized" genius. I tie that into Alexis de Tocqueville: Tocqueville is speculating about the place of genius in democracies and in societies of equality. He basically says that the towering figures will be harder and harder to find yet you'll have genius spread throughout a whole culture so that you'll have productive power and intelligence and so forth.

I think that we live at a time when it's hard to be invested in this idea that single individuals build companies or that single individuals come up with ideas that change the face of the globe.

On the one hand there's a cult that surrounds that kind of figure: Steve Jobs who builds Apple from scratch or what have you. But on the other hand we understand that it doesn't really work that way: all intellectual endeavour is social endeavour. Lots of people are involved in making great ideas.

And so the more that becomes evident, the more we realize that intellectual endeavour is social endeavour, the more appealing the myth of the great genius figure becomes. We've democratized genius so that we have geniuses everywhere. But when you do that, the single exceptional being cannot exist.

When I ask people to name a genius in the postwar world other than Einstein, I almost always get a pause but then eventually they'll come up with their own personal playlist of their favourite individuals from human history, and you may or may not share them. But Einstein is that last iconic genius in this sense. There are people who approximate that—Picasso, for example—but they tend to be holdovers from a previous era or they tend to be people who are just not widely shared: Richard Feynman was a genius of course but many people who don't have a science background wouldn't recognize the name.

HB: There's a great line about that in your book when you mention a documentary about Feynman entitled *No Ordinary Genius*. Which naturally made me think, *Hang on...*

DM: Right. There was once a time when that would have been a contradiction in terms, but that time is no longer. We have ordinary geniuses all over the place.

Questions for Discussion:

1. To what extent is it meaningful to make statements like "Our society is getting smarter"?

2. Do you think the term "genius" is overused? Underused?

3. Can you think of any "modern geniuses" other than Einstein?

VIII. The Future of Genius
Next steps

HB: So let's indulge in some speculation now.

There's this tension between the forces of equality which are forcing us to realize, as you say, that intellectual endeavour is social endeavour, and an older more romantic notion of the solitary transcendent genius like Einstein upon whom we might be able to pin our hopes.

Moving forwards 10 years, 20 years, 30 years, do you think there is room in our society, given the way it's presently constructed and how it's moving, for a new genius to emerge?

DM: Why is it that historians are always asked to prognosticate?

HB: I have barely begun my speculative requests.

DM: I have a friend at Columbia, Matt Connelly, who works on the history of the future. And one of the points he makes—and he's quite right to do so—is that in fact historically, historians thought about the future quite a lot. So when Thucydides is writing about the Peloponnesian War, he's doing so because he wants to learn lessons that can be applied to the future.

I haven't thought about this, to be honest: what is the place of genius going forward? I guess the easy response would just be a continual flattening.

HB: Yes, but you're not going to give me that.

DM: I'm not going to give you that, I'm going to give you something more exciting.

Well, I think it's pretty clear from both the book and our conversation that I have deep reservations about investing human beings with these kinds of semi-miraculous powers. I think in many ways the cult of genius has been a perverse development. On the other hand, as we were just discussing, I think there's a natural human longing to find the transcendent in the world and to find it in other human beings.

I end the book with a reference to Ralph Waldo Emerson, who has an essay that serves as one of the epigraphs, the *"Uses of Great Men"*, in which he gets at this tension in democracies: on the one hand we tear down the great individuals—which on the whole is probably a good thing—and yet we have a need for this kind of figure.

In levelling our society, we've cast aspersions on the whole notion of greatness. Academics, for example, can no longer use the word "greatness" without feeling uncomfortable. The demotion of genius in popular culture has been accompanied by a refocusing from the outstanding individuals towards the social basis that somehow creates these kinds of figures. All of which has been for the better in terms of how we study these things, and yet we've reached a point where we're uncomfortable with the very notion of greatness.

I think, on some level, maybe Western societies at least have lost the ability to make those distinctions. What is it that genuinely makes human beings great? Obviously to make those distinctions involves values and a calculus that we're uncomfortable with in this comparably relativistic age.

But I guess there's part of me that would like to see—I don't want to say the recovery of the cult of genius—but rather the recovery of the great individual (and I stress "individual" because the cult of great men has been just that; it's a gendered cult), great human beings who do more than simply bring a product to market, who do more than simply throw a ball farther than somebody else, who do great moral things, who do great intellectual things. I'd like to see a space for that again.

That reminds me, too, of something that Einstein said, which is very interesting. One of the reasons why he's such a hero in my book, as you alluded to before, is that he self-consciously deconstructs the cult of genius even as he inhabits it and lives it. That's problematic for him because he clearly uses his status to promote causes he's interested in.

He is, on some level, flattered: he enjoys being a celebrity to some extent and yet he's fundamentally uncomfortable with human hierarchy. But he has this one line where he says: *"If the world has to have geniuses, maybe it's better that it's people like me, who devote themselves not to amassing wealth and power but simply to pursuing the life of the mind."* He says that gives him faith that we don't live in such a materialistic time.

So, if we can recapture some of that, maybe that would be for the better. But I tend to be pessimistic with all things in life, so I'm not so sure that that's happening anytime soon.

Questions for Discussion:

1. Are we living in a "post-genius" age?

2. To what extent is "celebrity culture" compatible with the notion of genius?

IX. Gradually Expanding
Genius as cultural phenomenon

HB: That strikes me as an extremely reasonable and well-spoken response. As you were speaking I did think of one person who fits at least some of the aspects of a post-Einsteinian type of figure: Nelson Mandela. I'm not sure he would be regarded as "a genius" to be invoked in the same breath as Einstein, but clearly he is—quite rightly—viewed as an iconic figure, a transcendent moral beacon.

You also mentioned "the West" in passing—here we are, two white guys talking about all these things that happened in the past, in France, in Greece and Rome, and so forth. Are we now living in an age when there are opportunities—or perhaps it's even a reality—for people of a non-Western persuasion to be invoking the cult of genius?

DM: Clearly there are. This is one of the things that begins to happen in the 20th century. The science that emerges in the 19th century to try and explain genius is also a deeply racist science.

It's a science that has to have a continuum like a bell curve. On the one hand you have geniuses—who are always white European males—and on the other hand you have everyone else. So this whole notion of genius has this kind of shady past which I think one always has to be aware of when we talk about these concepts.

Nonetheless, from the 19th century forward there are successful efforts to challenge this notion. Gertrude Stein famously announces, "*I am a genius*". She says that self-consciously because she's flaunting this male-gendered cult and demanding recognition amongst the pantheon.

There are other people who are slowly admitted into it beginning in the 20th century and after the Second World War. The notion is expanded to include not just both genders but other races.

Are there brilliant, creative people in other parts of the world? Of course there are and there always have been. This is the other part of the story that I take pains to explain. If you think of genius simply as we often use the word colloquially: intelligent, creative people, well then there have been geniuses at all times and all places.

But the way the cult emerges—in contradiction to the new notion of human equality and at a time when at least one part of the world is being self-consciously disenchanted—*that* explains why the cult of genius emerges in Europe at the time and place that it does.

Not because there was a greater concentration of intellect there—that's a whole other discussion that certain people are willing to have, but not something I'm interested in—but because the social conditions allowed for the emergence of this figure in a way that didn't happen in China or India in the 18th century.

Those social conditions have now spread throughout the world—not everywhere and very imperfectly—yet people can now talk about disenchantment in various parts of the world even as we are witnessing a very powerful resurgence of religion in the public sphere. One can talk about an ethos of equality even in places where it's denied, and yet the idea is still there.

So I think that provides a new way of thinking about genius; and at the risk of veering towards the banal, globalization does enable a kind of back and forth to happen.

A famous example is Srinivasa Ramanujan, the great Indian mathematician who was fortunately discovered and brought to Cambridge by G.H. Hardy. That was a rare occurrence, but was the sort of thing that could happen in the early 20th century. Nowadays one could imagine him being able to study online for free and then get a scholarship to go to Cambridge.

HB: I certainly think it's important to emphasize that the modern cult of genius arose in a specific time and place due to specific circumstances. As you say, that's a different thing entirely from making sweeping statements about human intellect or capacity for achievement or anything like that.

DM: The other thing too is that the sullying that occurs with Hitler in the West happens elsewhere. Mao is the best example of this: he proclaims himself a genius in a lot of the propaganda and then he later takes it back because it rather contradicts Marxist theory.

I also write about Russia at some length, namely Stalin and Lenin, and the effort to study Lenin's brain and so forth. Again it's in fundamental tension with Marx's ideas.

In fact, Marx does write about genius, and very critically too. Yet no sooner has he got one foot in the grave than everyone's proclaiming him a genius, including Engels, who gives this famous speech at his graveside likening him to Darwin—that's part of the propaganda that emerges.

That too was very self-consciously instrumentalized and manipulated by the Soviets who also recognized the human need for these kinds of figures and used them in very insidious ways.

Questions for Discussion:

1. Do you regard Nelson Mandela as a type of "genius"? Why or why not?

2. Are there some cultures that are more susceptible to the notion of a genius? Less susceptible?

X. The Science of Genius
Brainology and other tales

HB: Anything left? Anything that I haven't said or that you want to add?

DM: Well, we haven't talked a whole lot about the science. One of the things that I try to do in the book, and in one chapter in particular, is show how when genius emerges in the 18th century as both a power and a person—there are geniuses, and geniuses posses genius—it raises the question, "*What is this thing that they possess?*" On the one hand that's mysterious by definition because part of the genius' role is to create mystery and be mysterious.

HB: But the business of science is to go the other way.

DM: Exactly. There's an ancient lineage for this, going all the way back to Aristotle, or more likely Pseudo-Aristotle, who writes a book called *The Problems* about the humours. He saw a common feature of great minds, a common physiological feature, in this older view. In other words: genius ought to be a force or power that you can apply to different things—you can use genius for statecraft or for generalship, for poetry, for science. So what *is* this thing? This sets off this great scientific search that I light-heartedly call "geniology": the study of genius.

It begins in the 18th century in physiognomy with Johann Kaspar Lavater, the great Swiss physiognomist. He believes that if genius exists and if it's original—if you're born with it—you ought to be able to identify it.

So he studies it at great length, and that attempt continues right into the 20th century. I make an allusion to a German psychologist nominated for a Nobel Prize, who writes a book on men of genius that has 20 pages of plates of their faces. This was written in the 1920s.

So that's the earliest and in some ways crudest scientific study of genius, but then there's phrenology: the effort to read the bumps on the head. There are ironies here because in some ways the phrenological understanding of the mind is more in line with the modern understanding of the mind than the science that emerges afterwards. In other words, phrenologists believed that the mind was compartmentalized and that different features of the brain lend themselves to different functions. That view is rejected in the 19th century and phrenologists are thought of as pseudoscientists. But the science that emerges, craniometry, which is the study of the skull, has this very crude idea that the bigger the brain, the better. There's this effort in the 19th century to weigh the brains of geniuses.

HB: These guys went around hunting skulls, right? They wanted to fill their libraries with skulls, didn't they?

DM: They were literally digging them up. The skull of Immanuel Kant, the great German philosopher, is dug up in the late 1860s and studied very carefully and precise measurements were made.

HB: Well, it's easier to do that than to read the *Critique of Pure Reason* I guess.

DM: Exactly, you don't have to be a genius. You just get some calipers out and make a few basic measurements.

So there are great collections built. One of the greatest is still at the *Musée de l'Homme* in Paris, which was put together in the 19th century. Once again they were out there with calipers measuring size and shape until someone points out that if the size of the brain is related to the intellectual power behind it, shouldn't the whale be the smartest creature on Earth?

HB: There's certainly an argument for that.

DM: Well, possibly.

Of course all these embarrassing things become apparent because they start actually measuring the weight of the brains of some of these geniuses. Some of them, I think it was Turgenev, the Russian novelist, had this incredibly heavy head. But then other figures turned out to be rather disappointing, and that presents all sorts of problems, so you have to sort of fudge those numbers.

This leads to the development of the IQ exam, which is developed in France, not to identify genius but to identify retardation so that special-needs children can be singled out early on in their lives and hopefully get special training and support. But it's very quickly turned on its head and is seen as a way to potentially identify genius.

One of the points that I make in the book that I don't think has been really sufficiently appreciated by people who have studied this, is that this hunt for a marker of genius, the IQ, emerges directly out of this whole 19th-century "geniological" science.

Lewis Terman, the American psychologist I referred to before who spent most of his career at Stanford, builds on Binet's thinking and makes the IQ exam what it is and uses it for mass populations.

He's interested in genius from the very beginning. His doctoral dissertation is called *"Genius and Stupidity"*. Like Galton, who's one of his heroes, he's trying to figure out how you identify geniuses in a population pool. And he realizes—and he's right about this, of course—that the ability to do that would be of tremendous national security interest.

It's no wonder the Soviets are so interested in studying brains. They studied Lenin's brain, and there's still a brain institute that operates in Moscow.

So the Soviets are busy studying Lenin's brain and the brains of other Soviet geniuses so they can figure out how to reproduce this phenomenon. Of course, earlier on there was a whole eugenics movement in the Soviet Union.

Meanwhile, when Einstein died his brain was taken, against his explicit instructions, and preserved. There was great interest in Washington in studying it. There's an American scientist who actually studied Mussolini's brain, after his body is recovered, trying to find the genius, or the madness. He wants to study Einstein's brain too but the guy who took it won't give it to him.

So it's another confirmation, in a way, of the IQ exam's shady past.

HB: It seems like, speaking very broad-brush, there are two issues here.

There's the cult of genius, with all the history, sociology, politics, culture and all those other factors that can be brought into play to explain when notions arose and why, the etymology, what we mean by "genius", how it is used or misused in society and so forth.

And then there's this other question of: *What the heck is really going on?* Are there people who really are of exceptional. unprecedented ability, like a Mozart or an Einstein, who merit an entirely separate category? Does this label of "genius" actually, objectively, mean anything? After all, it's a scientific question whether there is a continuum in intellectual abilities or not.

And of course these two ideas overlap and intersect but it seems like at some level they are very different things. When you have the scientists who are looking at rigorously trying to do that, they're applying scientific techniques and trying to measure things and building their theories, but at the same time they're presumably under the influence of these psychological or political or historical beliefs.

DM: And sometimes the scientific theories are influencing them in ways they might not even fully appreciate. The study between madness and genius is very interesting in this respect.

It's an old association, which goes all the way back to the Greeks. The Romantics revived it and stylized it: the idea of the distraught, driven to distraction, obsessive, neurotic, mad genius is a Romantic type.

But then there's the science that develops in the 19th century—it was regarded as a science but we would call it pseudoscience—that tries to explain physiologically what's going on. And the science that emerges in France, and is picked up elsewhere, is called "degeneration theory". The idea is that genius is actually a kind of sickness, and one of its ancillary effects is creative brilliance.

You get this wonderful case—I love this story—of Émile Zola, the great French novelist, who regards himself as a genius, so he realizes that he must be mad on some level, but he doesn't want to be *too* mad. So he gets himself checked out by a panel of French psychologists who pronounce that he is, indeed, neurotic, but a high-functioning type of neurotic. In other words: he's not *genuinely* mad, but just enough so that he can wear the genius label.

So there's this whole silly sort of science that I talk about at some length, which is bought into by large numbers of people.

It turns out that in certain sectors like poetry you can understand that there might actually be a link. What do poets do well? They draw associations or metaphors between things that, to the outside observer, might be completely unrelated or extraneous. Well, if you push that same ability to an extreme you end at schizophrenia: the ability to make meaning out of the meaningless.

There are still debates about whether there's any kind of logic to these arguments. You can see how it can work in certain sectors but clearly in others madness and genius wouldn't go together at all. Galton, back in the 19th century, wanted to deny this connection altogether. He says: "*Look, geniuses are, on average, robust, healthy, sort-of supermen creatures*", and that's what Terman reiterates.

But the principal point is that you get this old association of genius and madness that also feeds into this religious notion of genius as a kind of exalted seer who is singled out and overtaken by this possessive power—literally this divine fury or enthusiasm—and who is capable, just like the ancient Sybil, the Oracle at Delphi, to make these prophetic and profound statements. So the science confirms a kind of religious, prophetic notion that further enhances the aura of the genius.

HB: That's a great point to end on. Thank you, sir. That was a lot of fun.

DM: It *was* a lot of fun. You know, I probably did 300 interviews for the Happiness book, and one of the things that you learn very quickly is that there's a kind of interview where you talk to someone and the producer has given them the sheet 15 seconds before they go on the air and it's really a kind of painful, laborious process.

Then, there are the kinds of interviews like this one where you have a really good conversation and you sharpen the way you think about things in the process, or in response to questions you're forced to think about things that you hadn't been asked before. So thank you, it was a genuine pleasure.

Questions for Discussion:

1. Would it be a good or bad thing for science to develop a complete understanding of what makes somebody intelligent?

2. If there were a pill you could take to increase your intelligence, would you take it?

Continuing the Conversation

Readers who enjoyed this conversation are naturally referred to Darrin's book, *Divine Fury: A History of Genius*, as well as his other works: *Happiness: A History* and *Enemies of the Enlightenment*.

Turning the Mirror

A View From the East

A conversation with Pankaj Mishra

Introduction

The Weight of History

Sometime shortly before my eighth birthday, I had my first personal taste of the legacy of history. I was visiting Mont Ste. Anne just outside of Quebec City and found myself sitting beside someone on a chairlift who went out of his way to make me feel inadequate because I was unable to successfully communicate with him in French. To him, clearly, I was yet another in a constant line of imperialist anglophones cavalierly encroaching upon his land.

Of course I was nothing of the sort: I was just a middle-class kid from Toronto on a family ski holiday. But the whole experience made me feel both ashamed at my linguistic inadequacy and indignant that I was somehow being held responsible for historical events that I wasn't even loosely associated with. *What*, I can remember thinking defensively, *had any of this history business to do with* **me**?

It all seemed monstrously unfair. After all, it wasn't as if I was even *indirectly* responsible, a proud descendant of British military veterans who had served on the Plains of Abraham. As it happened, when the Battle of Quebec was going on, my ancestors weren't speaking English or French. And yet, irritatingly, none of that seemed to matter. To my tormentor that day I might have been General Wolfe himself.

Mind you, there is oppression and there is oppression. If the Québecois are justified in putting *Je me souviens* on their license plates, it does rather make one wonder what sort of appropriate response the Chinese might be entitled to after having suffered the unrelenting series of imperialistic subjugations from the Opium Wars to the Rape of Nanking.

There are no hard and fast rules here, no well-established scale of history's burdens. But one thing is abundantly clear: it is not enough to protest, "*I wasn't there!*" or "*This had nothing to do with me!*"

Because not having been there isn't the point. What matters is to both remember and actively seek some understanding of what has occurred: a careful, studied reflection of what has gone before is the primary way we can elevate our present circumstances beyond that of a seemingly random series of disconnected events. It is not just "context"—although of course it is that too. It is an opportunity to experience a real sense of perspective, real empathy, real understanding.

In *From the Ruins of Empire, The Intellectuals Who Remade Asia*, celebrated writer Pankaj Mishra, provides us with just such an opportunity. By closely examining the work and impact of a small number of highly influential Asian thinkers of the mid to late 19th and early 20th century, Mishra does more than simply shatter trite stereotypes of "East vs. West", he gives us a real sense of empathy of what it was like to be living at that place and time.

> "*One of the impulses behind the creation of the book was to excavate certain ideas, certain ways of life, certain worldviews that we have tended to neglect if not suppress or ignore altogether: to look at what, say, a Chinese intellectual in the late 19th century or early 20th century, was thinking when confronting this enormous challenge of Western imperialism or Western capitalism. That kind of challenge was really existential; and my book is really about individuals at particular stages in history, looking at the world around them, seeing existential challenges everywhere.*

> "'**How can we hold on to the society we've had and its traditions— particularly literary traditions, cultural traditions—that have been around for a very long time? How can we hold on to those, while also living with dignity in the wider world?**'

> "*So imperialism becomes a very important factor for all of these people, because what it is asking them to do—whether you're in India*

which is physically occupied by British imperials, or in China or the Ottoman Empire which is not physically occupied but nevertheless feels this enormous pressure from the West—is to radically transform their societies, completely overhaul them in order to become strong enough to survive in the wider world. Otherwise your lands, your territories, your cultures, will be even more dominated by the West than they already are.

"That, really, is a challenge that I wanted to describe in this book: how did people respond to it?"

Developing a heightened sense of empathy for those who face urgent existential challenges to their long-held way of life is one thing, but the first reaction I had at picking up *From the Ruins of Empire* was a rather more personal one: a profound sense of embarrassment that I knew virtually nothing about any of the people being written about.

That, too, of course, is a sign of the problem, an indication of just how long overdue a deliberately Asia-centric account is. For when I told Pankaj of my distinct sense of discomfort at being so bluntly confronted with my profound ignorance of these Asian thinkers, he assured me that I was hardly alone.

"Actually a lot of people said that; this was a very common reaction. And the important thing here is that I was no different. If you'd asked me six or seven years ago who Liang Qichao was—China's foremost modern intellectual—I would have said "no idea". I wouldn't have had any name recognition.

"So this is a measure of the ignorance that even someone who grew up in India has about the culture and history of China, an immediate neighbour and one of the most important countries today.

"But this is a manifestation of how our knowledge systems are structured—the way we think of ourselves and the world, the way we look at the world—which is a way almost entirely framed by Western social sciences and the way history has been taught in academia for the last 150 years or so. So that whether you are in India, or whether you are in Toronto or in France or in London, there is a certain

> *kind of history you grow up reading. And that history excludes so many, many different aspects of our common experience of the last 150 years or so, because they're all kinds of nationalist histories. If they're not nationalist histories then they tend to be imperial histories, and imperial histories exclude even more than nationalist histories."*

But just because you might receive the same type of education as your average Westerner, that hardly means that your personal experiences will be similar.

> *"If you grew up in a world like Allabahad, you're really surrounded by crisis, by breakdown, continuous breakdown. And that's really been the experience for me growing up in India: being surrounded by crisis and a kind of modernity that is unachievable, unattainable—a sense of having arrived late in history.*
>
> *"This is something that haunts us all: missing the boat, and then being forced to adopt certain ways, certain methods. And even if you succeed in your own life, you find that other people around you are failing. Really, what you see around you is evidence of massive overwhelming failure—even if you grow up in a relatively large city like Delhi or Mumbai, that sense of crisis never really leaves you.*
>
> *"I think that is one difference I feel increasingly between people who grew up in places like Turkey or Egypt or India and people who have grown up in the West at a time of prosperity, at a time of great power for the West, where their assumptions are informed by national power, their sense of national strength, and the fact that their model of modernity is being imitated."*

I am, of course, one of those very people whose fundamental sense of modernity has been framed so differently from that of Pankaj, to likely permanent effect. But having had the chance to read *From the Ruins of Empire* and then talk with him about it afterwards has nonetheless gone a considerable way towards giving me a much deeper sense of understanding of a very different world that was created in the shadow of a very different type of history. Which is, at least, a beginning.

The Conversation

I. A Different Perspective

Unknown intellectuals and overlooked worldviews

HB: There were three distinct impressions that I had after reading *From the Ruins of Empire: The Intellectuals Who Remade Asia*. The first was a sense of being confronted—in a rather unpleasant and yet captivating way—with my own ignorance. I found myself reading about people whom, quite frankly, I had never heard of before. I like to think of myself as a reasonably cultivated person, yet here's this book that's talking about the profound influences of various Asian intellectuals who were completely unfamiliar to me.

I had never heard of Liang Qichao or Sayyid Jamal al-Din al-Afghani before I read your book. I *had* heard of Rabindranath Tagore, but only the name—I had no real sense of who he was or what he had done. At any rate that was my first reaction.

The second reaction I had was related to the whole issue of colonialism. If I'm honest, I'd say that I hadn't thought about it very much beforehand. I suppose my thinking was that there were good and bad aspects associated with colonialism: a certain level of infrastructure was laid down, while clearly, at the same time, a considerable number of moral transgressions occurred. All in all I didn't have terribly strong views on the matter. But I came away from reading your book with a much stronger sense that this was just an egregious moral wrong—there was no more any level of ambiguity whatsoever for me: this was a really crappy thing that human beings have done to one another.

My third reaction was a certain queasiness about what all this means today and where we can, and should, go from here. Hopefully we'll get back to this later on in our discussion.

But I'd like to start off by asking you about my first response that I just mentioned, about being swamped with feelings of ignorance. Was this a common reaction? Were there others who felt, *Gosh, I really should have known more about this*, or, *It's quite embarrassing that I didn't know anything about the history of this part of the world at this point in time?* Did other people come away with that sense too—or am I, somehow, the only one?

PM: Actually, a lot of people said that—this was a very common reaction. And an important point to make here is that even me, the author of the book, knew very little about these characters before I started out.

Had you asked me, six or seven years ago, who Liang Qichao was—China's foremost intellectual of the late 19th and early 20th century—I would have said "no idea." I simply wouldn't have had any name recognition. This, then, is a measure of the level of ignorance that even someone who grew up in India, in the part of the world we call Asia today, has about an immediate neighbour, about the culture and history of China, one of the most important countries today.

This is a manifestation of how our knowledge systems are structured—the way we think of ourselves and the world—which is a way almost entirely framed by Western social science and the way in which history has been taught in academia for the last 150 years or so. So that whether you are in Toronto or France or London, there is a certain kind of history you grow up reading. And that history excludes so many, many different aspects of our common experience of the last 150 years or so, because they're all kinds of nationalist histories. And if they're not nationalist histories then they tend to be imperial histories, and imperial histories exclude even more than nationalist histories.

So I think that level of ignorance you mentioned is fairly common; and actually one of the reasons why I wrote that book was to address, very specifically, that ignorance. That was one of the impulses behind that book.

The other impulse was of course to excavate certain ideas, certain ways of life, certain worldviews that we have tended to neglect if not suppress or ignore altogether.

HB: Such as?

PM: Well, to look at what, say, Chinese intellectuals in the late 19th and early 20th centuries were thinking when they confronted this enormous challenge of Western imperialism or Western capitalism—the kind of challenge that was really existential.

Mind you, I am not a professional historian. My book is really about individuals at particular stages in history, looking at the world around them, seeing existential challenges everywhere. They were very much characters in an existential situation. That is really what the book is about: How can we hold on to the society we've had, hold on to our literary and cultural traditions that have been around for a very long time, and also live with dignity in the wider world?

So imperialism becomes a very important factor for all of these people, because whether you're in India—which is occupied by British imperials—or in China or the Ottoman Empire—which are not physically occupied—you nevertheless feel this enormous pressure from the West to radically transform your society, completely overhaul it to become strong enough to survive in the wider world. Otherwise your lands, your territories, your cultures, will be even more dominated by the West than they already are.

That is a challenge that I wanted to describe in this book—How did people respond to it? What did they say, in the first instance? The book is almost entirely about the first generation of Chinese, Indian, Turks, Iranians, Egyptians, and so forth.

HB: But you draw links between them, over time.

PM: Yes, I do, because they looked at each other. They were not only looking at the West but they were also looking at other countries, other societies. They were looking at Japan, most importantly.

So it's important to examine that particular world of cosmopolitan exchanges and travels across Asia into Europe and America. We've become so accustomed to the West looking at non-Western societies, but we've really had no idea of how people from non-Western societies have looked at the West over the last 150-200 years. That was another motivation.

HB: There is this sense, then, of turning the mirror in the other direction.

PM: Absolutely, yes.

Questions for Discussion:

1. Do you share Howard's sense of ignorance of prominent 19th and early 20th century Asian intellectuals? If so, do you find it embarrassing or understandable—or, somehow, both?

2. How have your views on colonialism evolved? Do you think that there are positive aspects of the legacy of colonialism that should also be mentioned alongside the negative ones?

II. Demanding a Response
Reacting to an existential challenge

HB: There's also the question of what it means to be Asian or Eastern. Can one even talk coherently about "Asian values"? That's a question that I'm grappling with.

At the beginning of *From the Ruins of Empire* you talk about these major intellectuals who are responding to the West, or thinking about responding to the West, in three separate ways.

One approach is to say, "*We have to revert back to our own values*". This approach is manifested in movements like pan-Islamism, where there is a belief that, "*Our set of values is going to be triumphant and we shouldn't give in to Western thinking*".

Another approach, meanwhile, is a belief that these values should be tweaked somehow, that some things should be adopted from the West within a domestic overall value framework, while a third response involves an entire overhaul of the way to do things, as is evidenced by people like Mao.

I guess what I'm struggling with is this notion of a pan-Asian response being just that: a response, something done in opposition to the West rather than an affirmation of "Asian values", whatever that means. Of course, I appreciate that, historically, there were very good reasons for that. But in some ways I'm wondering if that doesn't cloud what it means to actually have these Asian values.

PM: Well, I think that's a very important question. One of the very important things here is to not essentialize. So when someone like Tagore, for instance—to take a very specific example—is talking about the values of Asia, the spirituality of Asia, one has to look at that as a very pragmatic invocation of certain values that Tagore thinks are being neglected in the Western tradition.

He credits the East with these particular values and says, "*These are also important, these are what we have embodied all these centuries; and for these values to be forsaken, for these values to be abandoned in the rush to embrace modernity, now that would be a tragedy*".

These invocations, then, of Asian values, of pan-Asianisms, are all happening in very particular historical contexts. They're very much contingent upon the degree of threat that most people, who are talking about these things, feel in their particular historical moment. So it's very important to see these invocations in the context of this very serious challenge by the West.

And as I keep insisting throughout the book, it's not just a political, military and economic challenge: it's an *existential* challenge, a spiritual challenge, because the particular model of society, the particular idea of the individual that Western modernity is proposing —and mind you these ideas are quite new within the West itself at that point—pose a very radical challenge to the way a lot of people in places like China have conceptualized themselves, have looked at their own place in the world.

So this is something really very, very new. To take just one example of what I'm talking about, there is a particular notion of "progress" in human affairs: that we are heading towards one particular place, that all of history is taking us to that one particular place and that we are all engaged in a journey towards getting there. This is basically a Christian idea—predestination—which has been adapted to various secular ideologies in the 19th century, whether it's free trade or later variances of communism.

This particular notion keeps being incarnated over and over again, together with various ways in which we can reach this particular destination: that the world should be made over in the image of Europe, whether it's the communists or 19th century British imperialists. It's basically this idea that the rest of the world has to resemble a small minority within Western Europe. And, of course, later the United States joins that picture.

If you look, then, at people in Asia in the late 19th century or in the early 20th century, this is what they're responding to: a universalizing universalism emanating from a small part of the world—a subset of Western Europe—generalizing itself around the world.

It's a fully developed set of ideas and ideologies that basically asks people to uproot themselves, overhaul their own traditions, and radically renovate themselves in order to survive in this world the West is making.

This is really how the question needs to be posed, which makes it inevitable that so much that has been said and written at that point will be in response to the West.

HB: By definition.

PM: Yes, by definition.

Questions for Discussion:

1. To what extent do you think most nations still believe in the notion of "progress" that Pankaj outlines in this chapter?

2. How do you think contemporary American-Chinese relations would differ had China not been subjected to Western imperialism?

III. Inseparable Factors?
Capitalism, imperialism and modernity

HB: I appreciate that the Asian intellectual reaction is necessarily a response to external circumstances imposed by the West—a necessary response to not only economic and political factors, but also an existential challenge to their very way of life.

And yet I'd like to try to parse things a little bit more, because, after all, there are many people in the West—there are people in Cincinnati and Birmingham, say—who are also having considerable trouble adapting to modernity.

PM: Absolutely.

HB: This question of how we should adapt to the world as it is changing, certainly affects all sorts of people in all sorts of different societies. So it seems to me you've got this legacy of imperialism, which is very strong and very damaging, and then there's also a recognition that the local economy needs to be fixed.

You have many examples in your book when intellectual leaders, politicians, other people on the ground, recognize that the society needs to be reformed—be it in China, or India, or wherever. There often seems to be an awareness of an economically damaging sense of listlessness.

So you've got economic competition through capitalism, the legacy of imperialism, and then this notion of modernity that is imposing itself. And it seems to me that at some level those are three different things.

PM: They're not different things, no. I think modernity arrives, in large parts of the non-West—not just in Asia but in Latin America and Africa too—under the auspices of imperialism; and for that reason, in the minds of many people it's tainted from the very beginning.

It arrives as exploitation. It arrives by self-sufficient food producers being forced to produce cash crops. The opium trade is a classic example of that: suddenly you have an entire country being forced to consume opium. And because the trade deficits are so high —like now, as it happens—you need to sell something to China, since China's the one country that's selling everything to everyone else.

If you see the logic of that—if you see the logic of capital, for instance, operating in these societies—you will see how it is very deeply bound with a worldview, an ideology, a philosophy.

In a Western context we think of modernity as a positive value, but one has to take on board the experiences of people who did not quite see modernization in that way, even though there were many benefits to be had by it, ranging from better medicine to greater agricultural production. But there were also many losses, while the fact that all of this occurred through coercion made things worse.

As you point out quite rightly, modernity is a very problematic thing for many, many people around the world. You had some horrible forms of exploitation in North America and in Latin America before these societies really began to enter modernity.

There's an entire literature of the late 19th century or the early 20th century in North America that is full of descriptions of that kind of exploitative capitalism. European 19th century literature is also full of that sort of thing, together with the Romantic response to it with people like Ruskin and others who have attested to this devastating quality of modernization and "modernity" in their own part of the world.

So if it was destructive in a part of the world that already had so many advantages—that had already conquered so many unexplored, unknown continents and had harnessed the resources of those continents for their own economic growth—if that kind of suffering and distress could be felt by people within Europe, just *imagine* its impact in parts of the world who had no continents to conquer.

And that's still the case for people trying to modernize themselves, for people trying to catch up with the West in this great race that was started in the 19th century. Large societies like India and China with large populations are at a huge disadvantage: they don't really have continents to conquer, commodities to have a monopoly over. They have to buy their way to their commodities, and they have to appease and mollify and bribe. And still it's not going to be enough—there are far too many people in those places.

I think this whole question of whether or not modernization was a good or a bad thing really has to be seen in the context of imperialism. It cannot be separated from these larger questions of how it was originally felt, and how it actually arrived in these places.

Questions for Discussion:

1. Do you agree with Pankaj that it is impossible to engage in a meaningful discussion of modernity in Asia without explicit reference to imperialism?

2. To what extent are China's recent resource-oriented policies in Africa relevant to the ideas discussed in this chapter?

3. Is modern capitalism necessarily exploitative?

IV. East and West

A meaningful distinction?

HB: Is there a real difference between people that are from the East—broadly defined, and we can talk in more detail about what that means exactly—and people from the West?

On the one hand, there's the view that, *Well no, we're all the same. It's all the human condition: everybody has the same needs and desires.* By this view, the only real distinction between Eastern people and between Western people are, what might be called, "accidents of history", various contingent events including the legacy of imperialism.

Another view, however, would be to say, *No, there are entire regions of the world where people really **do** have different values. They really **do** think differently and act differently; and we can, in some ways, assess those differences independently beyond just saying that they were a response to the West or a collective sense of feeling embarrassed or shamed.*

In your book you cited this penetrating quote by Tagore where he says, "*We all felt like defendants in a European court*". By "we all" he presumably was referring to some sense of Asian universality. So that makes me wonder, what ***is*** that, exactly? Is there anything more than a sense of shared victimhood from Western imperialism? Do you see where I'm going with this...?

PM: Yes, I think I see what you're driving at. If I've interpreted you correctly, you're asking a question about diversity, about differences: are there real differences?

HB: Yes.

PM: Is there a real diversity of outlooks, worldviews, ways of thinking, ways of feeling that can be clarified by these distinctions between East and West? I would say no. And I would also add that one has to move beyond these often very banal dualisms, because they obscure more than they clarify. I think you have to look at the logic of particular ideas: we have to look at the logic of certain processes that were set into motion in the 19th century.

The legacy of imperialism, then, is not just the backwardness, the perennial backwardness, of large parts of Asia. One of the legacies of imperialism is the rising economic strength of China today: the fact that so much of the Chinese attempt at self-consolidation, at self-strengthening, comes out of that particular history.

The fact that China has been underwriting the American consumer economy for a very long time is *also* a legacy of imperialism.

The fact that the East is now present in the West—the West has been present in the East for a very long time—is *also* a legacy of imperialism.

So if you want to isolate this, if you want to understand the situation, it won't help to look at it as purely an "East versus West" thing or as "China having their revenge over America". One has to look at this as part of a larger process of ideas that at one point in history originated from one part of the world, spread and transformed entire societies so as to give them a particular shape and set them on a particular historical trajectory.

That's really what we should be looking at, rather than imposing these dualisms between East and West, or even the North versus the South, although that has its uses.

It should be said that all of these dualisms have their uses: they can explain a few situations. How can you explain the late 19th century without talking about how these people responded to the West? Some of that dualism has to be invoked because so many of the people involved are obviously invoking it. How can you talk about underdevelopment without talking about the North and the South in the 20th century, how these countries were systematically de-industrialized, and in the post-colonial phase really struggled to get back on their feet again and re-industrialize themselves? Obviously, there were certain divisions that made it possible for many people at that time to posit this North versus South divide.

So all of these dualisms and binaries have their particular uses, but I think a more mature understanding of the world of the last 150 years really has to derive from an understanding of the particular movements and processes of ideas, of systems—of state-building programs, for instance. Take the whole idea of the nation-state. That could be one frame through which you could look at the organization of the world in the last 150 years: the nation state is a very modern thing.

And there's the fact that, as I described in the book, Japan becomes an imperialist power. That's also one of the legacies of imperialism: that the West arrives in the East, as it were, and the East "turns itself into" the West.

That is an interesting irony to follow—one that Tagore, of course, wrote about at great length. So it really is no longer useful to keep invoking these particular binaries.

In various other writings I've done, I've been regularly opposed to this notion that the West is something very unique, or the East is something very unique, and they all developed in isolation from each other, or stagnated in isolation from each other, or whatever.

This is really a kind of triumphalist propaganda that people come up with, on both sides, to feel good about themselves, to give themselves a kind of emotional moral satisfaction and moral gratification. But I don't think it's very useful.

HB: Well, let me push you a little bit more here. There is this notion, broadly defined, of the West, at least the West today as it's been for the last couple hundred years, post-Adam Smith, post-John Locke, wherever you want to draw the line. The standard story is that the ideology of the West is represented by individual rights and liberties—

PM: The property-owning individual.

HB: Well, OK. But the point is that this might be contrasted with more communitarian notions that are sometimes ascribed to Eastern views.

I remember some time ago people like Singapore's Lee Kuan Yew would regularly invoke this notion of "Asian values", claiming a greater sense of importance for communitarian beliefs as opposed to an individual-centric orientation.

Now doubtless there were many other agendas at play there, and likely still are, but I'm wondering if there was any truth to that perspective at all?

PM: That instance of various Asian strongmen, authoritarian figures invoking "Asian values", is merely an instance of a certain set of ideas being deployed very instrumentally—very deviously one might say—by various autocratic figures to justify their authoritarian views. One can safely dismiss those particular invocations of Asian values because they were very clearly justifying, vindicating, their authoritarian views by referencing these supposedly ancient values of Confucian ideas of harmony or community.

I think we should immediately describe that as an exercise in cynicism. There's not much there in terms of intellectual substance, in my view.

But if you take a specific society—like Japan for instance—and ask, *Is there a different sense of the self there? Is there a particular idea of individuality?* It's an interesting discovery that when you start reading Japanese novels, you notice that they're very distinctive. Some of them I name in *From the Ruins of History*, others I don't.

It's very clear that they have a very different idea of what constitutes individuality, or what constitutes a human self. They have a notion that is more duty-bound, more bound to the community at large. There are certain rituals, responsibilities and duties that really define the individual, rather than individual desires or motivations of the individual who is autonomous and independent of society.

Now, this is one syndrome you will see reflected in various degrees across many Asian societies, but not *just* Asian societies:

Latin-American societies, tribal societies, I mean, there's so much ethnography about this.

Someone like Claude Lévi-Strauss, a figure whom I often quote, spent his entire life uncovering certain structures of "the savage mind", as he called it, and the myriad ways in which different societies prioritize certain values above others, or strive to certain values while completely rejecting others that we, as supposedly modern people, uphold.

So I think there's always been that difference, which is not to say that within the West itself these particular notions of a more communitarian society—for want of a better word—have not existed.

HB: In pockets.

PM: Yes, in pockets. That's another useful way to look at it. As Proust once said, *"Everything that has been written about has been written about before. Everything that has been taught has been taught before. But since nobody listens, it's important to write those things all over again, think those things all over again".*

People like the Buddha—those with his worldview, who were sceptical of the individual, his desires, his autonomy—also existed in the West. If you look at the Western philosophical or political tradition, you'll easily come up with people who had ideas that were remarkably similar to those that the Buddha himself came up with—I talk about them in my own book about the Buddha (*An End to Suffering: The Buddha in the World*).

Now the important thing is that because of certain historical contingencies, certain ideas and traditions become more prominent, become the dominant tradition. Modernity is one of those traditions in the West that has suppressed so many other political, philosophical, and literary traditions.

And the fact is that if you bring those other traditions into dialogue with some of these Asian traditions and Asian figures, you will find a remarkable degree of similarity there. And let's not forget, people like Gandhi, people like Tagore, were educated and had their sensibilities informed by Western writers and intellectuals and thinkers.

So in many ways they are also conducting a dialogue with the West, it's not just this "modern West" or "imperialist West" but this *other* West that is not dominant within the West itself, outside of the Western mainstream. But it nevertheless exists; and this is what they're interested in talking to, and having a dialogue with, and learning from.

Questions for Discussion:

1. Do you agree with Pankaj that what is now largely regarded as "the Western tradition" is the result of certain "historical contingencies"? If so, what do you think those contingencies were, exactly?

2. To what extent does Japan's invasion of Korea in the late 16th century and centuries of Imperial China serve as evidence of a constant desire for conquest throughout all human societies?

V. Discovering Buddhism
Transcending false stereotypes

HB: I picked up your book on Buddhism, *An End to Suffering: The Buddha in the World*, after I had read *From the Ruins of Empire*. Again a somewhat uncomfortable admission: before I began reading, my notion of Buddhism was of something indisputably and exotically Eastern—the only overlap there seemed to be with my own, shall we say, Western background involved images of drugged-out guys in California that made it all very hard to take seriously.

It seemed very mystical and other-worldly: there were elements of reincarnation and prolonged meditation in uncomfortable positions—in short, it all seemed pretty wacky, and completely opposed to anything that a rational, reasonable, pragmatic, serious individual would ever want to consider in his or her life.

Perhaps I'm not painting myself in the best possible picture, but that was, briefly put, my perspective. So when I picked up this book and started reading it, I became shocked by how you regularly compare and contrast some of the key aspects of Buddhist philosophy with all sorts of Western thinkers throughout history—people like Nietzsche, Dostoyevsky, and Baudelaire, to name but a few.

"*Well, OK*", you might say, "*This Mishra is a clever fellow who can make all sorts of different connections to different literary and cultural traditions*", but the thing that really overwhelmed me was the sense of *pragmatism* of the Buddha. In your telling of it at least, he struck me as more of a psychologist than anything else, concerned with basic, universal aspects of the human condition. *How can we end suffering? How can we live a better life and triumph over our often meaningless questing?*

There's none of this strange metaphysical business of heaven or hell, these eschatological constructs that we would associate with Christianity, Judaism, and Islam and most of us have become so inured to that we've stopped being able to fully appreciate how truly weird most of them are. There's none of that.

In fact, there's even a passage somewhere, if memory serves, where somebody asks the Buddha some metaphysical question and he remains silent. And when they ask him, "*Why did you remain silent?*" he replies something like, "*Well, I have nothing to say about this, so I'm saying nothing at all*".

Once again, I was struck by a real sense of pragmatism about how to fruitfully live one's life, and I was also struck by the universality of the message: there are some really important teachings here that are appropriate for people independent of where they live or which culture they might broadly associate themselves with.

Perhaps I'm getting carried away, but it left a fairly deep impression on me because I took several courses in philosophy years ago, and I thought to myself, *How is it possible that you can get an entire degree in philosophy in the West and come away from that experience not being exposed to these ideas at all, simply consigning all of Eastern philosophy to some sort of hugely inappropriate "flaky" category?* That seems pretty bizarre, in retrospect.

PM: Well, that's one of the incompatibilities of these disparities that we've talked about earlier: that so much about the history of the world, so much of the history of philosophy, was originally framed in Western academia. So whoever goes through that system, and its extensions in various other parts of the world—almost all university systems are very much modelled on those of the West—will come away with not really knowing much about non-Western traditions of moral and political philosophy. And you would be naturally inclined to have that perspective that you had about those hedonistic Californians, which is essentially that all other approaches are a waste of time—it's an excuse for laziness and parasitism of some sort or other.

But the fact is that there have been some incredibly sophisticated ideas—some very interesting notions of consciousness and how the mind works—articulated two and a half millennia ago. This comes as a revelation to most.

Nowadays there are neuroscientists working on Buddhist thought, and there are any number of very ambitious projects underway to examine the links between modern scientific discoveries about how the brain works and what the Buddhists have been saying all along about the way the mind works. But the fact is that we often don't know about these things because certain traditions have been de-emphasized, suppressed, and ignored.

If you were to ask me what my role is in all this, I see it as primarily one of self-education: I have to educate *myself* in the first instance. I didn't know anything about the Buddha, although I grew up in India—I was born there. This is also the country where the Buddha was born, where he spent most of his life, but I didn't know anything about him. So this was an education for me, a discovery I had to make for myself.

And then I ask other people to share in it, because I think that it might be interesting to them as well. The same impulse went into *From the Ruins of Empire*. Here, again, we have fascinating figures, but neglected, obscured. And it's high time that we look at what they were saying, how they saw the West at a particular time, how they saw their own societies, how they saw human possibility in general.

So that's very much where the Buddha book came from. I thought that it was important to take a close look at this man who, two thousand five hundred years ago, described change that was being confronted in his world.

These changes were very radical by the standards of that world: close knit, community-minded societies becoming urbanized, with many people moving to larger cities giving rise to larger urban settlements that were coming into place all across North India. And with this came into being new ideas as to how the human self was to be described. It's a time of intense religious and metaphysical speculation. And the Buddha emerges in this context.

This society also contained a great deal of violence. So he's meditating on all these problems, and he arrives at this notion that the human individual, or this claim upon individuality and autonomy, is actually very shaky. What is the individual? Where do these desires come from? And do these desires really lead to fulfillment, or just lead to more desires?

So he starts with these basic questions, but there's also this sense that the human being—and the Buddha shares this with a lot of other religions and philosophies—is not, by himself, an admirable figure: he's someone to be extremely wary of.

The Buddha would consider our ideas of Western humanism, Renaissance humanism or Enlightenment humanism very dangerous.

He would be deeply sceptical of this exaltation of the human as a source of wisdom, a source of reason; the notion that someone is capable of a great deal of tolerance by thinking rationally would strike him as a very bogus idea.

And so much of the history of the last two hundred years has borne that out.

Questions for Discussion:

1. Do you agree with Howard that Buddhism is regularly associated with notions of "being alternative" in Western society? What do you think of when you hear the word "Buddhism"?

2. Pankaj seems to be making a clear connection, if not an equivalence, between the terms "Western humanism", "Renaissance humanism" and "Enlightenment humanism". Is that justified? To what extent is it reasonable to say that "humanism" is equivalent to an exaltation of human beings?

3. Are most university humanities curricula too Western-centric?

VI. Personal Examinations
Growing up Western in the East

HB: Let me explore your personal situation a bit deeper. You have very strong roots in the West—not only because you live here, but as you've mentioned repeatedly, your primary intellectual influences were clearly Western. You're steeped in the Western tradition, and yet at the same time you have very strong senses of what it means to be Asian.

PM: Well, I'm not exceptional in that regard. Any number of Indians, Egyptians, or Chinese, say, would be extremely well-versed in the Western tradition because that's what we're taught at school, that's what we're told to really absorb if we want to get on in the modern world.

This is something you grow up with if you belong to the right class—even if you're from the lower middle class, in fact—you have to do that simply in order to get ahead. It's not something that you choose to learn.

In the West, on the other hand, you have to make a conscious choice to learn something about India or Egypt. It's not really necessary, it's not necessary to your well-being or material success in the world, as it is in India. And that's a really crucial difference.

We grew up with the West as this thing you have to learn about and master. Speaking the language is very important if you want to be a part of this world of material success, even if you want to simply survive—I'm not talking about wanting to be a millionaire—even if you want to get a poorly paid job somewhere you have to learn the English language.

So the West for us is not a choice, it's a compulsion. We need to learn about the West and master some of its historical, philosophical or literary traditions.

The other part—feeling Eastern—is often actually the more difficult part, because in many instances we experience an uprooting of sorts. Even though we live in different parts of Asia, we're actually quite disconnected from those traditions—as you can see, for example, in my not being aware of the history and the philosophy of Buddhism until quite late in my life.

Now, why was this? I spent so much of my life very close to the areas where the Buddha was born, where he preached, where he moved—and yet I knew nothing about it.

So much of my education in the last ten to fifteen years, which has been a type of self-education, has really been in these philosophical and literary traditions of Asia.

It's not that I feel torn between the two, because that assumes that the traditions of Asia—or the traditions of India for that matter—are something that I'm already steeped in. I'm actually not. I know a lot more about the West at this point, about Western literature, about Western philosophy, than I do about large parts of the Asian tradition.

But the challenge, the stimulating thing, is that there is so much to learn, so much to discover. We've only really started discovering the histories, philosophies and literatures of a large part of the world. It's incredible how really West-centric we've been. I'm not just accusing people of the West of being West-centric, but *we*, in Asia, have been deeply West-centric. And very slowly we're beginning to emerge from this fixation, from this obsession, and beginning to learn to look at ourselves, at our own societies, at our own traditions. Often those traditions are mediated through Western philosophies or Western ideas—but this is how knowledge proceeds, how knowledge develops.

HB: And, for that matter, Western researchers themselves. You mentioned in *An End to Suffering* how some aspects of Buddhist philosophy were rediscovered through the work of Western thinkers, and some of the ironies that were involved there.

PM: Yes, exactly.

HB: I guess what I'm really trying to get at is a sense of where you resonate in terms of your particular values. It's one thing to say, "*Well, I had to learn all these things, I had to read all these things, because that's what they were teaching at university, and that's what I had to do to get a job; those were the expectations in the society where I was living*". But it's another thing to say, "*These particular things, these particular viewpoints, intrinsically hold some personal value for me*".

PM: Well, in that sense it's been enormously enriching. So even if there was an original compulsion to learn about the West, it has immensely enriched my life and made possible the kind of intellectual journeys that I now engage in.

I don't see how I would have even begun to study the various Indian traditions, or Buddhism, or Chinese philosophy, without that background, without that kind of training. That's really important.

Now, if you're asking me if there is a particular set of values that I subscribe to that are particular to any one part of the world, I would say no. I can find them in various traditions, in various figures, in various thinkers, whether it's someone like Nietzsche—whom I cite a great deal in *An End To Suffering*, sometimes to underline the astonishing similarities between what he was saying in the 19th century and what the Buddha was thinking about in 5th–6th century BC—or whether it's Lévi-Strauss or Simone Weil, whom I don't quote so often but who has been a huge influence on my thinking about various issues, although she wrote very little.

These figures, whom I keep reading and rereading, are very important to me, as are those in the traditions that I've only begun to discover, be it the Chinese tradition, or Indonesia. Again, I'm looking at sympathetic figures.

HB: So what makes them sympathetic in your view?

PM: I think one thing that unites them all, and which makes them very compelling figures for me, is their sense of a world in deep crisis and radical transition. This is what they're attesting to, this is what they're really talking about.

I'm not attracted to people who are writing at a time of great prosperity and well-being. I'm not so keen on, for instance, the Renaissance philosophers, who were talking about statecraft and various aesthetic theories that were being formulated at that time.

I'm not so keen on the Enlightenment philosophers—they don't really speak to me. There are certain Western philosophers who *do* speak to me because they are talking about a time, a world, which resembles my own.

If you grew up in a world like Allabahad, you're really surrounded by crisis—by breakdown, continuous breakdown—and that's really been the experience for me growing up in India: being surrounded by crisis and a kind of modernity that is unachievable and unattainable—a sense of having arrived late in history. This is something that haunts many of us, haunts us still.

HB: Missing the boat somehow.

PM: Yes, missing the boat; and then being forced to adopt certain ways, certain methods. And even if you succeed in your own life, there is the concern of finding other people around you who are failing.

And really, what you see around you is evidence of a massive overwhelming failure—all around you, if you grow up in those parts.

Even if you grow up in a relatively large city like Delhi or Mumbai, that sense of crisis never really leaves you. That is one difference I increasingly feel between people who grew up in places like Turkey or Egypt or India and people who have grown up in the West at a time of prosperity and power, whose assumptions are informed by their sense of national power and national strength and the fact that their model of modernity is being imitated.

Now, in what particular way is it being imitated, and what are the consequences of that around the world? Well, nobody knows. But nevertheless a lot of people want to imitate that. They want to be, if not physically in America, just like Americans, or at least they want to *consume* like Americans.

That creates a certain kind of worldview, a certain set of assumptions, which inform a certain outlook and a worldview that has its own integrity.

Now, if you were born in India or Turkey in the last century or so, you would have a very different sense of these processes. There is a very strong sense of crisis for those who have lived in these countries with a history of civil wars, coups, people fighting each other for state power, growing nationalisms, and tribalism.

There is a very different sense of the world altogether. And in that context the people you'll naturally respond to, the people you find sympathetic, are those who've also experienced that similar sense of crisis.

Questions for Discussion:

1. What intellectual or cultural traditions would you like to be more familiar with and why?

2. Do you agree with Pankaj when he says, "I don't see how I would have even begun to study the various Indian traditions, or Buddhism, or Chinese philosophy, without that background, without that kind of training"? To what extent is it necessary to have experience in any one particular cultural or literary tradition in order to understand another?

3. How can we be certain that a past writer is living in a world that "resembles our own"? Is it reasonable to talk about people "writing at a time of great prosperity and well-being"? Do such categorizations make sense when considering writers with individual sensibilities? In what ways does Friedrich Nietzsche serve as a counterexample to such a view?

VII. At an Impasse
The end of an experiment

HB: You talked movingly just now about "a sense of crisis" felt by many people growing up in a place like India or Turkey. How do you feel when you hear the words "economic crisis" being thrown around repeatedly in the wake of the events of 2008? Do you have an urge to stand up and shout from the rooftops, You people have no idea what a crisis is really all about! Or do you think about it somehow differently?

PM: I think crises are good ways to reexamine many of our assumptions, many of our belief systems that we've unconsciously and unthinkingly embraced. And if this crisis, which is now a prolonged crisis—it's been going on for five years now, with no end in sight—provokes new thinking, new ideas or reflections then that is a good thing.

What does the history of Europe or the world over the last 150 years or so have to teach us? Have there been suppressed ideas embedded in these different genealogies of Europe or in America that we need to excavate and bring up to light again? I'm talking here about basic questions like, *What is the good life?*

And those questions are being asked now.

HB: Are they? Do you *really* get a sense of people digging down and asking profound questions that have long been suppressed? Because I don't, I have to tell you.

PM: Well, I see them more than I did, when, seven or eight years ago, I toured the United States with my Buddha book and met bemused audiences everywhere. That was a time where the stock market was booming and things were going well.

The Iraq war was a bit of a disaster, but the economy was still doing great and there was certainly no sense of crisis. Now I find a very different kind of response altogether when I meet large audiences or when I go out and meet people. There's a different kind of questioning that is reflected in any number of intellectual trends, whether it's the invocation of Marx as a very effective critic of capitalism, or people saying "*Well, let's look at Bhutan, they've figured out a way to measure happiness—*"

HB: And not just measure it: apparently they actually *are* happy there.

PM: Yes, perhaps.

We need to look at other ways of measuring the health of our societies: it's not enough to just look at GDP growth or infant mortality rates or various other standard measures—maybe there are other indicators. In different ways, then, there's this sort of churning now that you see being manifested in this sort of thinking. Obviously there's a lot more to come, and there should be.

I really think we're at an impasse at this point. We really have come to the end of a very long experiment, which was this experiment of modernity: that it could be universalized, that billions and billions of people would all have the same lifestyle, would all have the same kind of outlook, would all have the same sort of worldview, and consume more or less in the same kind of way.

We've come to the end of that, simply because there's this little question of nature to be considered. Planet Earth has become a major critic of our various ambitious, fanciful, ideologies and ideas. It's telling us that this can't go on. It just can not go on.

So I think that whatever new ideas come out of this moment are to be welcomed, because unless you experience a crisis, you have not had this moment of reckoning.

HB: Do you see any genuinely new ideas coming out? I agree that there's certainly a growing societal awareness of environmental degradation, but other than that, I'm not sure I see much in the way of radical new thinking. Do you?

PM: Not at this point, no. Especially if you're thinking of it from the perspective of the man on the street, the reader of newspapers for instance, you would not get that sense at all.

Look at the press, the legislature or the judiciary—these are highly conservative institutions. We have a long way to go before we see any new thinking emerge, let alone new thinking turning into actual policy. These institutions all thrive on these older unsustainable models.

This is subject matter for an entirely separate discussion, but just look at how journalists have become part of the elite. This is an extraordinary phenomenon and we haven't even really noticed it: how they've become the mouthpieces for businessmen and politicians. There is any number of examples: look at how the *New York Times* or any major newspaper in the Western world supported the war in Iraq, for example.

HB: There's not much objective critical thinking going on.

PM: No. If you look at the profiles or the backgrounds of some of the major journalists, commentators and observers, where are they spending most of their time? Who are they hanging out with? Who are the audiences they're addressing? They're all addressing *each other*—in Davos or Aspen or wherever. They're all talking to the elites.

HB: And they're self-proclaimed elites. I mean, they're not even genuine intellectual elites by some standard objective measure.

PM: That's right—absolutely. So I think what we're looking at is a rapid circulation in these circles of bad knowledge, of defective knowledge, and it's very, very hard for alternative forms of knowledge to break in. Whether they should get into those circles is another matter altogether—

HB: Why shouldn't they?

PM: Well, the thing is there's not much point in telling a corporate CEO who's thinking of setting up more factories in Indonesia, "*Look Mr. CEO, most of Sumatra has been devastated already by palm oil prospectors and so much of Java has been lost to rampant industrialization and tree felling. So please don't do this there*".

HB: It's going to be a waste of time, presumably. If any change will occur, it's going to come from some form of regulation.

PM: Absolutely—and why would the government regulate? If you look at the UK for instance, you see a situation where the Chancellor of the Exchequer is basically battling to save the salaries of corporate executives that the EU is proposing should be cut. He doesn't want them to be cut. Why? Because how will they be funded, if not by the City? I'm talking about the Tory government in this case, but I don't think a Labour government would behave very differently in this regard.

So everywhere you look, you look at nexuses, you look at collusions, entrenched interests. It's very difficult to imagine how the government enforces any regulations, let alone brings them into play in the first place.

Questions for Discussion:

1. Is the media's "rapid circulation of defective knowledge" significantly worse today than it was when this discussion took place in 2013? How might we improve upon it?

2. Is modern capitalism compatible with responsible environmental policies?

VIII. Learning From the Past
The benefits of increased historical understanding

HB: I'd like to return to the matter of my queasiness I alluded to at the beginning of our conversation. Basically, my problem is this: granted that horrible things happened in the past under colonialism, and one could say that with the rapid economic development of China it's "payback time" to some extent, but what does all that really mean? I mean, isn't the key question, How can we move forwards in a constructive way based upon a new, richer, awareness of what has happened?

Speaking personally, I now have a deeper understanding from reading your book of what has transpired during colonial times, together with some sense of the principal Asian thinkers who were trying to move forwards, some more successfully than others. But now what do I do? And how can I, with this knowledge, somehow constructively use it to make the world a better place?

That's a bit trite, and I realize that it's also not your responsibility. But I'm talking to you, and you've obviously thought about these issues, so I thought I'd ask: where do we go from here?

PM: Well, I'm not a prophet. But as a writer, I feel my responsibility is to point people to particular aspects of our past which have not been written about, which have been ignored and neglected, and to encourage them to explore those aspects much, much deeper.

The important thing is that all our histories, whether you're in the West or in the East, are full of instances of journeys not taken, roads not taken, alternative modernities never really explored.

Perhaps it means asking, *How can we arrive at a political unit without all of us embracing the nation-state? Can there be an alternative to the nation-state that does not cause as much suffering, say, for ethnic and religious minorities?* Now, those are questions Europe also has to ask of itself.

HB: Far more than it is presently doing, in fact.

PM: Absolutely. So all of these questions, and the answers to them —or at least *some* of those answers—have to come from an exploration of our different histories, whether it's the history of Asia before the nation-state or the history of multi-ethnic and multi-religious empires such as the Ottoman or the Qing. These are not all rosy histories to learn from, but one does not really learn from history in that kind of banal way.

There are instances, however: there are interesting moments when you can say, "*Ah,* **this** *is a better model of coexistence than what we have come up with*".

It's important to develop a historical awareness that, *This is also how people once lived upon this earth: they were also violent, they were also greedy and selfish, but they devised certain political and economical mechanisms whereby those negative tendencies could be controlled and contained and the damage from them could be limited.*

That is what I, in my own very modest way, am trying to do: to point to particular instances of this—or even just to people who talked about those particular instances—and say, "*Well, we just can't stand here today and say there is no alternative but to go down this path of collective suicide and destruction of the planet*".

We just can't do that. That would be the worst kind of intellectual dishonesty, because there have been human societies before us, centuries and centuries of them, with their own ways of being, with their own ways of living.

And this is what, I think, as a writer, I can do: I can simply point to them.

HB: And hopefully efforts like yours will also make people a little bit more tolerant. Let me try to be more concrete and tell you one thing that occurred to me as I was reading your book and getting a more consistent sense of the horrors that a country like China was subjected to for a prolonged period of time.

I found myself imagining being steeped in that history myself, being forced to swallow a couple of centuries' worth of unmitigated aggression from all sides—from imperialist gunboat diplomacy and the Opium Wars to the invasion of Japan—and then having to listen to the standard sanctimonious utterances of an American Secretary of State, say, about human rights violations or environmental degradations.

Now one has to be very, very careful. I believe that there *are* human rights violations that happen in China and I believe that they are indefensible. I am **not in any way** saying, "*You can't make an omelette without breaking a few eggs, and some human rights violations are a reasonable price to pay as you're moving forward with the greatest economic experiment in mankind*".

I'm not saying that at all. But what I *am* saying is that there has to be, I think, a greater understanding of putting oneself in the other person's position, appreciating the full historical context of the situation at hand.

So without being an apologist at all for any of those very real and pressing transgressions, I think that it's important to try to engage in a process of understanding what people on the other side of the fence, as it were, might be feeling. And I think books such as *From the Ruins of Empire* go a great distance to give people such a broader perspective and a broader understanding.

PM: Well, I'm glad you say that, because we commonly credit literature with the virtues of empathy and understanding by the ability to put the reader in the place of a particular character—sometimes, indeed, a character with largely negative aspects. And yet there's a certain sort of understanding fostered if the novelist is a very skillful one in understanding why that person is so horrible, so destructive or violent.

Now, there's a kind of account of world history that can be written, and indeed is written, which can also put the reader in a similar perspective of understanding how certain historical characters, certain historical actors, acted the way they did. Which is *not* to condone their actions or justify what they did by reference to some higher morality of national growth or national strength or whatever, but simply to understand what was acting upon people.

Mao Zedong, a great monster in Western demonology, tried to make China catch up with the West as quickly as possible in the 1950s, attempting to industrialize in double-quick time; and in the process committed some of the biggest calamities ever in the history of mankind—the Great Leap Forward and the famine that flowed from it.

Now, *that* was a great crime. But if we want to enlarge our understanding of how these crimes were committed, and what the logic was behind them: what was weighing on this man's mind—and, indeed, the people that were acting with him; he was not alone, he was not just a sole autocrat—then we have to understand what went before him. What were the particular pressures on this person at that time, and how did they produce such a ghastly result? Why did China become such an insular and aggressive country all through the 50s, 60s and 70s? And why, then, did it open up? And why does it still remain a prickly, nationalistic country?

So even to achieve a very basic understanding of international relations, books of this kind, histories of this kind, are important.

HB: They give you a context.

PM: Yes, they give you a context—without, again, divvying up the world in these camps of "the East" and "the West", but instead by simply looking at how these processes work.

You see the same process at work in Iran: the Shah of Iran modernizes brutally, and then a reaction against him comes in the form of the Islamic Revolution. You can see that in Turkey, you can see that in any number of countries across Asia. The same processes are at work: the imperatives of national self-strengthening, national consolidation giving rise to the emergence of an autocrat who basically suppresses all opposition, then the opposition has a coup and things start all over again—this whole cycle.

At one level this is the understanding that books like these can advance: you simply try to address what were the particular, specific, pressures upon individuals making decisions, momentous decisions.

You ask questions like, *What were their specific motivations at that particular time?* rather than sitting back and judging, *They're not like us—we who have arrived at the summit of prosperity and affluence of this glittering civilization dedicated to liberalism and human rights; and these people are so below us, so deprived of simple understanding of what liberalism and human rights mean—how can they do this?*

At the same time, one has to be very critical of countries like China, of authoritarian societies in particular. But you have to understand that the crimes that they've increasingly committed against their own people—and you have evidence of this sort of thing in India too against the Kashmiris or the Northeastern tribal peoples—is all in obedience to this particular logic of competitive economies, competitive nation-states. It is in keeping with this notion of competition as the basis of human existence, which is the new idea that emerged in the last two hundred years or so.

HB: Thank you very much, Pankaj. Is there anything you'd like to add or embellish upon before I let you go?

PM: No, actually I think we've covered quite a bit. Good questions, thank you. They made me think.

Questions for Discussion:

1. Do we pay sufficient attention to trying to understand the motivations of major historical figures rather than simply opting to "demonize" them? For an added perspective on this issue with respect to human rights abusers, see Chapter 5 of **Improving Human Rights** with UC San Diego human rights specialist Emilie Hafner-Burton.

2. To what extent do you think that a deeper historical understanding helps us collectively navigate our way out of current crises?

Continuing the Conversation

Those who enjoyed this conversation are naturally directed to Pankaj's books, *From the Ruins of Empire: The Intellectuals Who Remade Asia* and *An End to Suffering: The Buddha in the World,* that were referred to throughout the discussion.

Readers are also encouraged to sample some of Pankaj's other works, including: *Bland Fanatics: Liberals, Race and Empire, Age of Anger: A History of the Present* and *Temptations of the West: How to be Modern in India, Pakistan, Tibet and Beyond.*

Pants on Fire

On Lying in Politics

A conversation with Martin Jay

Introduction
The Varnished Truth

We all do it from time to time—dissemble, fib, fabulate, prevaricate, call it what you will—but for most of us, it all boils down to just one word: lying. Of course, not all lies are the same. From little white lies to moral necessities to bald-face deceit, there is a seemingly limitless spectrum for the lying-sensitive to explore.

Unsurprisingly perhaps, lying is also a recurrent literary and cultural theme, from Pinocchio to Oscar Wilde, Kafka to Shakespeare. Lying is, for better or worse, an essential aspect of the human condition.

Martin Jay, Ehrman Professor of History at UC Berkeley and one of America's most renowned intellectual historians, has also spent much time thinking about lying. But for Martin, examining equivocation is not so much motivated by a desire to probe our underlying moral framework, but rather to shed some light on the political animal within: might we be able to use the act of lying to help us better understand what separates the political domain from any other?

Intellectually primed by the likes of Jürgen Habermas, Friedrich Nietzsche and Hannah Arendt, Martin's mendacious musings began in earnest when asked by the *London Review of Books* to critique both Christopher Hitchens' anti-Clinton polemic *No One Left to Lie To* and George Stephanopoulos' memoir, *All Too Human*.

> "Writing those book reviews was the immediate cause. But there must have been something prior to that, which was probably my reading of Hannah Arendt, specifically her essays on truth and politics and lying in politics. These essays were in a way typically Arendtian—which is to say, against the conventional wisdom, provocative, and not

fully clear on the implications. She was always subtle enough to understand the ambiguities of positions. The notion that there is something special about the political realm—something that sets it apart—was something that she was a great advocate of.

*"Reading her essays started me thinking about whether or not one of the things that **did** set the political realm apart is precisely the "pass" given, under many circumstances, to the fudging, or twisting, or shading of the truth—and perhaps even to outright lying. At the very same time the accusation of lying—the accusation hurled at one's enemies—is itself such a staple of politics.*

*"That paradox—that people often accept the fact that politics is a realm in which certain moral conventions about lying are, if not suspended, at least qualified, while at the same time accepting that within politics the accusation of lying could be used as a tool against enemies—was probably lurking in the background when I began writing that article for the **London Review**."*

Several years later, Martin presented his continually developing ideas in the Richard Lectures at the University of Virginia, the core content of which was eventually published in book form as The Virtues of Mendacity: On Lying in Politics.

His conclusions, as usual, were many and varied.

First off, there is the question of "to whom the truth is owed":

"Politics involves interactions with people who are basically either adversarial or who have different interests. Politics involves getting something done or preventing something from getting done. It is inevitably consequentialist. The issue is to whom the truth is owed, and for what reason.

"Obviously, in a situation of full antagonism—a war, even a cold war —we don't owe the enemy the truth. There's no question that we want to win, and our existence may be at stake. Truth is always a casualty of war, for good or for ill. When we're fighting a war, we even propagandize our own people to try to lift their morale.

> *"Now, in somewhat less adversarial situations—in, let's say, a diplomatic situation, where we are jockeying for position but without violence or the threat of violence—there is a way in which we also know that there is a certain bending of the truth. You promise things, you sugar-coat things. The line that Sir Henry Wotton is always credited with— "A diplomat is an honest man sent abroad to lie for his country,"—captures that quality of our being in a kind of game, a political, international game of trying to gain advantage through whatever means—which sometimes includes lying."*

A parallel issue to consider, Martin asserts, is the equally significant notion of the "directionality of truth-telling": whether it is imposed from the powerful to the powerless or the other way around.

> *"Think of the Quentin Tarantino movie Inglourious Basterds, which begins with the 'Jew Hunter' coming to a house with his Nazi troops and asking a peasant, who is hiding Jews in the basement of the house, whether or not there are any Jews there. The peasant initially lies, trying to save them, protect them. But, finally, he is coerced through threats into telling the truth and the Jews are gunned down, with one of them escaping. In this case, there is a question of whether it would have been more moral to tell lies to power, to tell lies to the authorities. This is an example of the 'murderer-at-the-door' case."*

Indeed, the closer one looks at the political, the more complicated the situation seems to become. Do we really want our governments to tell the truth at all times? Are lies necessary for effective diplomacy? Is there something somehow positive, in short, that lying gives to politics, something we would be foolish to cut away, if we somehow could?

> *"The crucial thing is to think of the wariness that we have about lying as something that we can't give up. We ought not to be completely cynical about it. My book argues against the notion that politics is just the realm of self-interest, of corruption, of cynicism. It urges that something good gets done, even when people suspend overly moral, regulative ideals."*

In keeping with the great intellectual historian tradition to which he has so consistently contributed, an overarching conclusion to Martin's measured explorations is that things are vastly more subtle and complicated than they are often presented to us as being: that however unsuitable knee-jerk Manichean reductions to "good truth-tellers" and "evil liars" might be to our personal lives, they are likely even more unsuitable still to the political realm.

So it's complicated. But just when you least expect it, from all this nuanced analysis and subtle shades of grey, comes a specific political recommendation for everyone:

> *"The one lesson that comes out of this is to be more attentive to the substantive issues and less concerned with the character and truth-telling of the person who is defending them.*
>
> *"Sometimes scoundrels produce good outcomes, and sometimes pious, well-intentioned people produce lousy outcomes. One has to be aware of the fact that the person who beats his chest and says, '**I am the truth-teller. I am authentic. The other guy is the liar**,' may be basically leading us down a garden path. This is not to say that character counts for nothing, but we shouldn't vote for saints. We should vote for people who will produce outcomes that are beneficial. That is more important: substance over style."*

Now that, I'm convinced, just has to be true.

The Conversation

I. A Fruitful Approach

Investigating "the political"

HB: I'd like to discuss aspects of intellectual history and your other academic interests, and we will hopefully move in that direction during the course of this conversation. But for the moment let's begin with your book, *The Virtues of Mendacity: On Lying in Politics*, and discuss the motivations and inclinations that you had in writing it.

You start off the book by talking about Christopher Hitchens and his book on Bill Clinton, *No One Left to Lie To*. In that book, Hitchens alludes to lying and perjuring as the sine qua non of disreputability, along with why it is that no one should take the Clintons seriously. This piqued your interest not simply with respect to general attitudes towards lying, but to the entire issue of lying in the public realm.

Years later, when Hitchens became an advocate for the war in Iraq, the matter of whether the authorities had publicly lied concerning the existence of certain weapons of mass destruction, and other matters did not seem to matter to him so much anymore, as the justification for the war focused much more narrowly on the need to rid the world of Saddam Hussein. He tacked quite wildly himself.

But I'm guessing that you had been thinking about these sorts of ideas well before then. How much did Hitchens and his discussion of lying in the public sphere trigger things that were already there, and how much of that caused you to think afresh about these ideas?

MJ: Well, I doubt I would have written the book if I hadn't been asked by the *London Review of Books* to write a review of Hitchens' book. That was the immediate cause. But you're absolutely right, there must have been something prior to that; and it was probably my reading of Hannah Arendt, specifically her essays on truth and politics and lying in politics.

These essays were in a way typically Arendtian—which is to say, against the conventional wisdom, provocative, and not fully clear on the implications. She was always subtle enough to understand the ambiguities of positions. The notion that there is something special about the political realm—something that sets it apart—was something that she was a great advocate of.

Reading her essays started me thinking about whether or not one of the things that *did* set the political realm apart is precisely the "pass" given, under many circumstances, to the fudging, or twisting, or shading, of the truth—and perhaps even outright lying. At the very same time, the very accusation of lying—the accusation hurled at one's enemies—is itself such a staple of politics.

That paradox—that people often accept the fact that politics is a realm in which certain moral conventions about lying are, if not suspended, at least qualified, while at the same time accepting that within politics the accusation of lying could be used as a tool against enemies—was probably lurking in the background when I was asked to review the books by Hitchens and George Stephanopoulos by the *London Review*.

HB: It seems to me that, as an intellectual historian, this is a perfect sort of subject to wrap your head around, because you can look at not only lying but at the conjunction of lying and politics. You can explore that combination from Plato's time up to the present day, which of course you do in the book.

Am I wrong in saying that this is a paradigmatically meaty topic, one that as an intellectual historian you say to yourself, *"This is a good one. I can really sink my teeth into this"*?

MJ: Intellectual history gives you certain tools to relativize absolute contemporary positions. It gives you a sense of the sedimented and often contradictory legacy of other people's thoughts on these issues. So instead of thinking that you can ever get it right in the kind of transcendental way in which history is suspended, it makes you sensitive to the fact that other people, over many centuries and in many different contexts, have also thought about the same issues.

Lying itself, and the issue of what constitutes politics, are not questions that have self-evident answers. One has to do the spadework to figure out what other people have said.

I've always been interested in what I call "cultural semantics"—ways in which words mean different things over long periods of time, etymologies, and how different discursive contexts shade them in ways that we sometimes forget, but which, nonetheless, may still be palpable beneath the surface, still have an efficacy.

There's an enormous tradition of people pondering the implications of lying, the justifications—or lack thereof—for lying. And then, when I really got into this subject, questions about "the political"—what we mean by "politics", how we are to understand its boundaries, whether or not we can talk about it having an essence, whether or not we can make a distinction between "the political" as an ontological phenomenon on the one hand versus banal, mundane politics on the other—all of that became available for intellectual historical exploration.

HB: From my perspective, it looks like you used lying as a tool—as a scalpel, say—to look at what the political realm really is and how it differs from other areas. You talk about "leakage" from one realm to the other, while other political philosophers have sometimes spoken about "sealing off" a political realm. The question of lying seemed to me like a probe that you could use to explore these issues. Is that right?

MJ: I think that one could get into the political in many different ways. You can examine specific institutions, asking whether or not there are particularly political institutions as opposed to economic, social, or religious institutions, trying to determine when these political institutions became relatively autonomous (they're never fully autonomous).

One can ask about activities: what constitutes being political? Is the personal political, as we thought in the 1970s? If so, is there no distinction between a man deciding to wash the dishes or going on strike and starting a revolution, since everything is political?

You could also ask about the political in terms of its, as it is sometimes referred to, "oppositions in a semantic field": the public versus the private, the political versus the economic, or the political versus the moral.

Politics—and this is true of all terms—needs to be situated in a dynamic force field of competitive and sometimes synonymous terms. And the crucial thing to note is that this is historically variable: the political in our society at this moment is not the same as the political in the European Middle Ages, or in, say, a society that existed prior to Columbus' discovery of America.

These terms have their histories and they have their shifting terrains. As you say, one way to deal with that is to look at a particular theme. And for me, lying proved to be particularly fruitful in that respect.

Questions for Discussion:

1. Do you think that the political realm is a fundamentally different one than other areas of human activity? Are some people "naturally cut out for politics"?

2. What do you think Martin means, exactly, when he refers to "getting it right in the kind of transcendental way in which history is suspended"? Does this imply that there is no such thing as "objective truth"?

II. The Liar's Stage
From Machiavelli to political play-acting

HB: Another notion that you discuss is not only how different societal trends grow and recede, but how often specific concepts are actually misused or perverted, ascribed meanings that they did not originally have.

Machiavelli is a case in point. Depending on the time one lives in, and depending on where one is, he is either incredibly insightful, deeply realistic, the devil himself or something else entirely. You look at this—again, with the eyes of an intellectual historian—not only to show how ideas are received in a particular society, but to illustrate specific aspects of the backdrop to that society, what its cultural values are.

MJ: Machiavelli is a fascinating case. I should say at the outset that I'm certainly not a serious student of Machiavelli and the incredible body of literature that has been devoted to him, but he was clearly a thorn in the side of a lot of traditional positions in politics, religion, and morality. What he represented in perhaps a creative way was a recognition that the political—the state—could be autonomous in a way that made it no longer subordinate to religious and moral imperatives.

What we see in the modern world, especially after the Treaty of Westphalia that ended the Thirty Years' War, is a growing sense that religion and transcendent morality has to be kept at bay, and maybe even suspended, when it comes to *raisons d'état*: the self-justification of state-building and state survival. Machiavelli was one of the first people to put his finger on that. For people who like this idea, he could be hailed as a figure who understood the autonomy of the political and its relative freedom from external limits, such as those produced by religion or traditional morality. But this meant, of course, that he was construed as amoral by those who wanted to bring those moral constraints back.

HB: But from the perspective of mendacity, it seems to me that the interesting meta-comment to make is that Machiavelli was widely perceived as telling the truth, the naked truth. He wasn't dressing things up, he wasn't prettying them, he wasn't ascribing higher moral tendencies that we all know deep down might not actually be the case. He was telling the truth.

And within this broader context of questions concerning what it is to lie, what it is to tell the truth, who is telling the truth, who is lying, this brings out several interesting points.

MJ: Well, there are many paradoxes. There is the one you just alluded to: telling the truth about lying, or the truth about artifice, or the truth about the fact that culture trumps nature, or the truth about the fact that language is always deceptive rather than fully representational. We might call it "truth-telling about the fact that there is no truth". Nietzsche and others have played with this paradox.

But there is also the higher-level meta-reflection on the fact that being a truth-teller in this sense is *also* a ploy—is also, in itself, an artifice. This is an old idea that many deconstructionists, in particular, were keen on telling us about: the idea of *parabasis*, in which the Greek protagonist in a tragedy would suddenly take his mask off, turn toward the audience, and speak, as it were, from the heart. The protagonist would, in other words, move beyond his theatrical character and become, somehow, a person talking to you. But, as the deconstructionists point out, this was *itself* a trope, this was itself a ruse.

HB: That's what politicians do all the time. They say, *"Let me tell you straight: this guy is lying!"*

MJ: Exactly. And then they add, "*But **I'm** going to be authentic.*" So, this—we might call it "the pose of authenticity" or "the pose of being a truth-teller"—becomes *itself* part of the game, rather than somehow breaking the rules of the game. And Machiavelli, in a way, is part of that dialectic as well.

HB: You mentioned earlier your love of etymology. At some point in *The Virtues of Mendacity* you talk about where the word "hypocrisy" comes from. Apparently it was extracted from the Greek idea of "response", and it comes from the theatre—or, at least, it's related to the theatre—which is very interesting, because it alludes to the idea that what you see on stage is not real and not to be trusted: it's an act, it's an artifice, it's dressed-up.

And that seems to be a metaphor for the whole notion of artifice: *Who's telling the truth? Who's using fancy words? Who's on stage? Who's dressing up?*

MJ: I think it's amazingly complex. You're absolutely right: there are parallels between hypocrisy on the stage—where it's clear that people are play-acting—and lying in the public realm. Indeed, we use theatrical metaphors to attack politicians, by saying things like, "*He's only playing politics.*"

So there is a parallel; and yet, there's also a crucial difference between theatrical fiction and real life, which is that in real life a lie is meant to deceive and is based upon the trust you have with the person who is not doing the deceiving. Performatively, the real-life lie is designed not simply to describe something incorrectly, but rather to make you believe that I am telling the truth. Whereas on the stage, we know that we are in an aesthetic frame. We know, for instance, that the person on the stage is not really killing somebody.

HB: There's a suspension of disbelief.

MJ: Exactly. There is that interesting non-parallel quality: that it's theatrical, **but**. Real lives are at stake in politics, while real lives are *not* at stake in theatrical performances. There is a funny way in which there is an overlap, without a full identity, between the two. Lying is so serious because it has subjective *and* performative implications very different from those produced by fictionality that is understood by everyone as such.

HB: And there are, of course, people who have deliberately blurred that distinction, blurred that line. You mention, as just one example, *The Decay of Lying* by Oscar Wilde. He's playing with that whole notion.

MJ: Right. Exactly.

Questions for Discussion:

1. What do you think of when you hear the word Machiavellian? What do you think Machiavelli himself would make of the term were he to hear it used today?

2. To what extent does our common use of terms like "the political stage" or "the game of politics" reflect a deeper societal awareness of some of Martin's points in this chapter?

III. Lies, American Style
A central concern?

HB: Moving on to the United States: there's this whole mythos about looking at truth-telling as a direct, puritanical response to the former British colonial powers—to the aristocrats who spoke in fancy words, who had command of rhetoric. This has imbued itself in the public consciousness of the United States to such an extent that you still see aspects of it today. To me, that is particularly fascinating.

I'd like to focus for a moment on the American context and potential American exceptionalism. I had a discussion with your colleague David Hollinger not too long ago (*Battling Protestants*), and we were talking about the cultural influences in the United States that were derived from the puritanical ideas of its founders.

And I think that this can be seen again in some of the things that you write about in *The Virtues of Mendacity*. Perhaps the image that comes quickest to mind is one that everyone has heard of: the young George Washington, who cannot tell a lie, admits to cutting down a cherry tree. Here is this new country, this new society, and one of its founding myths is that its first president, its first leader, is incapable of lying.

Now, there are all sorts of interesting aspects to this. One of them is that, as you astutely point out, is that the story itself turns out to be a lie, a myth.

But what is striking is that the very invocation of this myth historically quite deliberately reinforces a concrete point of demarcation for the United States, a point at which Americans effectively say, "*We're starting anew, we're cutting ourselves off from the Old World with its hypocritical traditions. We're redefining the universal rights of man, and, consequently, we're going to do things properly in terms of governance and politics: no more lying, full transparency."*

Would you agree with that? That the public condemnation of lying has always played a particularly critical role in defining American cultural and political life?

MJ: I'm not an American historian, and I'm always loath to make very broad generalizations.

HB: Well, I'm not a historian at all, and I've already made quite a few. Go ahead: take the plunge.

MJ: I think there certainly were tendencies in American political and cultural life to demonize what they saw as the artifice of, say, European—maybe British—politics and culture, and a desire to start fresh in a New World in which one had experiences that were not pre-filtered through customs and traditions that would somehow be constraining.

The United States had this hope—innocence, we might call it—of clearing away a lot of the debris and beginning with a clean slate. This involved plain-speaking, it involved trying to overcome the deceptions associated with political and other types of life.

Now, one might argue that before the Civil War, the American South still maintained a strong sense of the importance of a kind of "courtly deception". And certainly the slavery question, if you think seriously about it, was one that the United States did not handle with transparency and with a real concern for truth-telling. The three-fifths clause in the Constitution is clearly a mendacious way to consider human beings: when Jefferson and others said that all men are created equal, there is a kind of asterisk. Suffice it to say that we weren't truth-telling in all respects.

But there were certainly moments of that in American history. My former student, the late Ken Cmiel, wrote a wonderful book on plain-speaking in the late nineteenth century in America (*Democratic Eloquence: The Fight over Popular Speech in Nineteenth-Century America*) that dealt with a desire to overcome what was seen as pomposity and circumlocutions and all the kinds of highfalutin language of traditional politics: to speak from the heart and be as accessible and inclusive as possible.

Now, this happens in Europe during a slightly later period—the great example is, of course, the war poetry of World War I, which begins with a kind of high rhetoric, the diction of classical or neoclassical tradition. And then, because the war is so disillusioning and disabuses people of these false expectations, poetry itself becomes much more direct, much more prose-like, much more along the lines of, *"Let's get rid of this garbage and talk from the heart."*

So various cultures at various points decide somehow that all this artifice, all this ornamentation, has to be gotten rid of. You find it in Europe in architecture, for example, with Adolf Loos, saying "Ornament is crime."

HB: Another example that comes to mind is that of George Orwell, who clearly was deeply insightful in terms of recognizing the abuses of language, criticizing people for all sorts of rhetorical flourishes that were superfluous and misleading. You point out that there is an irony there as well, because Orwell, who was constantly portraying himself as the representative of the common man and plain speech, was *himself* an intellectual, and was thus to some extent actually being somewhat duplicitous—ironies certainly abound.

MJ: Yes. So there are moments in virtually *every* culture where this becomes important.

HB: Sure. But those are specific periods, as opposed to the central American mythos, a defining ideal that I referred to earlier.

MJ: Well, there's something to that. We generally think of ourselves as being more straightforward in our self-presentations. All those books that I listed at one point in *The Virtues of Mendacity* that talk about lying show that we are still very uneasy about the fact that people, from the age of Barnum on up, are huckstering us, pulling our leg, deceiving us—politics as advertising. That undercurrent is definitely there.

Questions for Discussion:

1. Do you think that Americans focus on lying more than any other country?

2. In what ways do you think that the concept of "political transparency" is structurally linked to lying?

IV. Transcending Kant
The value of nuance

HB: As I said before, my thinking is that you're looking at lying not only as an interesting topic in the history of ideas, but also, perhaps even more significantly, as a tool to shine a light on what politics actually *is*: how is it that we can tolerate lying in one area and not in another, and what does that imply about politics?

What are some of the conclusions of your investigations?

MJ: Well, of course, there are many. One that I think is salient is the question of to whom the truth is owed.

There is a general presupposition that lying can be self-defeating and corrosive to one's soul. People like Augustine and Kant, who held strong anti-lying positions, have argued that, no matter the circumstances, as a liar you are sullied by your refusal to be truthful. For these people, then, *you* are the issue.

In politics, it's not so much about saving my soul. It's not so much about being pure. If I wanted to do that, I'd go become a monk. Politics involves interactions with people who are basically either adversarial or who have different interests. Politics involves getting something done or preventing something from getting done. It is inevitably consequentialist.

The issue is to whom the truth is owed, and for what reason. I looked at a wide spectrum of what we consider to be part of politics. Obviously, in a situation of full antagonism—a war, even a cold war—we don't owe the enemy the truth. There's no question that we want to win, and our existence may be at stake. Truth is always a casualty of war, for good or for ill. When we're fighting a war, we even propagandize our own people to try to lift their morale.

Now, in somewhat less adversarial situations—in, let's say, a diplomatic situation, where we're jockeying for position but without violence or the threat of violence—there's a way in which we also know that there is a certain bending of the truth. You promise things, you sugar-coat things. That line that Sir Henry Wotton is always credited with—"*A diplomat is an honest man sent abroad to lie for his country*"—captures that quality of our being in a kind of game, a political, international game of trying to gain advantage through whatever means—which sometimes includes lying.

HB: That's equivalent, it seems to me, to something you were saying before regarding being on stage and the suspension of disbelief. These are the rules of the game, as it were.

MJ: Exactly. Diplomacy has certain rules. That was why the Snowden revelations were so damaging: because we discovered that, for instance, the American ambassador to Germany was cabling home that he thought the German Minister of Defense was a fool. He wouldn't say that to the Minister of Defense, he wouldn't say it in public or in the newspapers. That was his job: to tell the truth to his superiors back home, but not to tell the truth to his German counterpart or to the public. But there was something shocking about seeing that unvarnished truth.

Another area that has distinct rules about truth-telling is domestic politics, where there is an adversarial relationship between competitive parties in a pluralist system. The Democrats don't tell the Republicans all the things they're thinking, and vice-versa. And we know that. There's a way in which we understand that the game involves strategic spins, strategic ways of manipulating the truth.

When President Obama disclosed that he didn't have a strategy for dealing with ISIS, everybody jumped on him for being so frank. Somebody—I think it was Michael Kinsley—said, "*Look, a gaffe is when a politician tells the truth.*" I think we're aware of the fact that in those circumstances, adversarial relationships are always problematic for truth-telling.

An additional question is whether a politician in office should lie to the people, lie to his constituents, lie to the people who trust him. Clearly you can't do this too much. Lying can't be normative—it can't be the default position. You have to have a reputation for truth to even get away with a lie.

But under certain circumstances, lying for the benefit of the people—to prevent, say, a panic on the stock market, or to rally morale, or to do something that at least in the short run is necessary—can perhaps be justified. Politicians do this all the time. We read their memoirs years later and they explain more frankly what they were doing. We know this.

It's an issue of trust: not so much blind trust that politicians will tell the truth, but trust that they are acting in a way that will benefit us. Occasionally, as is the case with a parent or a doctor, we trust people to think of our best interests rather than to just always tell the truth.

Now, the other issue that is absolutely crucial in politics is the *directionality* of truth-telling: from the powerful to the relatively powerless, or from the powerless up—from those who are threatened by the need to confess, the need to be somehow frank if the authorities demand something.

Think of the Quentin Tarantino movie *Inglourious Basterds*, which begins with the "Jew Hunter" coming to a house with his Nazi troops and asking a peasant, who is hiding Jews in the basement of the house, whether or not there are any Jews there. The peasant initially lies, trying to save them, protect them. But, finally, he is coerced through threats into telling the truth, and the Jews are gunned down, with one of them escaping.

In this case, there is a question of whether it would have been more moral to tell lies to power, to tell lies to the authorities. This is an example of the "murderer-at-the-door" case.

We all know now that the imperative to be honest can be problematic because of surveillance. The realm of privacy, the realm of "*I don't have to tell you; you don't have a right to know; I don't owe you the truth!*" means that if, for instance we are asked by the government to reveal for which party we voted in a secret ballot, we can't be forced to give up the truth, we can't be compelled to tell the truth in the old inquisitional model of being compelled.

But there are various ways now in which that is under threat, as we are forced by technology to give up truths that we might not want to disclose. So in some ways, the ability to lie in politics, the ability not to tell authorities what they want to know, sometimes saves us from being overly available to a certain coercive measure. Once again, it's very contextual and consequentialist and nuanced.

On the other hand, there are times when the government *does* want to know something, and they'll do something in a juridical context. You can appear before a congressional committee, for example, where you'll swear to tell the truth, the whole truth, and nothing but the truth. There, you are obliged to tell the truth.

But politicians—and this is one of the points I make in the book—when they take an oath, that's not the oath they are asked to attest to. They are not asked to say, "*I will tell the truth, the whole truth, and nothing but the truth.*" They may uphold the Constitution, but not that particular oath.

HB: And there is some understanding of a social covenant at play here. That is to say that there's an awareness among the populace that politicians are not actually swearing to tell the truth, the whole truth, and nothing but the truth. That's part of this directionality business that you're talking about.

MJ: Exactly. We want them to tell us the truth, but we don't always want them to tell the public or the enemy the truth. It's very variable. There is no rule. What comes out of a book like this is an awareness of how contextual and specific these kinds of situations really are, that there is no absolute rule that you must follow.

That's where Kant, I think, went wrong—in trying to oblige us through a transcendental rule that was somehow applicable no matter the circumstances.

HB: He also had space and time wrong.

MJ: That's a whole other conversation.

Questions for Discussion:

1. Can you imagine an occasion when it is impossible to "uphold the Constitution" **without** *telling a lie?*

2. What do you think has been the impact of "the Snowden Affair" on American and/or international politics?

V. Coming Clean
Appreciating what we know

HB: So there's the notion that things are rather more nuanced, less law-like, when it comes to lying than we might have first thought. Are there other conclusions that we can draw as well?

MJ: Well, lying has, as Hannah Arendt pointed out, a kind of forward-looking direction. You can lie about facts in the past, but they're very hard to undo. As someone once said, you can lie about many things, but you can't make Belgium the country that invaded Germany in 1914. It just didn't happen. Lying about the past is hard.

Politics often involves the future: "*I promise that if I'm elected, I'll do this,*", "*Watch out—if this guy gets in, he'll do that.*" You make these conditional statements with your fingers crossed.

There are lots of ways in which politics involves making statements about what will happen in the future, which are statements more of hope and intention than of fact. Therefore, they have built into them a kind of—not fully lying—but at least an openness to the possibility of it going in a totally different direction.

Politicians can't be explicit about this. They have to say, "*If I get in, **this** is going to happen: elect me and I will put a chicken in every pot.*" And yet, they know their promises are highly unlikely to be fulfilled, because the circumstances are not such that they are likely to get their way.

HB: They know, yes, but the populace also knows.

MJ: Well, if it's clever enough and has enough experience, the populace knows. But it often foolishly believes these pie-in the-sky promises. An awareness of the fact that politics is a game of ifs and conditional possibilities rather than law-like regularities and natural causality is a wise lesson to learn. I think that recognizing politics as part of that game is part of wisdom.

The other thing, of course, is that politics involves, if not utopian, let's say, *imaginative* hopes for something that might happen. Politics is the realm of desire, the realm of *We have a problem, let's fix it; we have an injustice let's right it*.

Lying is therefore also a way to argue against the dead weight of facts, against, *This is the way it is; this is the way it must be; this is the way it always has been*.

Often—and this is where we come back to artifice, theatricality, and fictionality—politics has within it the capacity to imagine what is *not* the case. Now, you do it in such a way that you claim it really *will* be the case—so there is a kind of obvious deception in it—but there is also some way in which it involves the belief that we can make the situation otherwise.

As I point out in an early chapter of the book that deals with nature and socialization, when children learn to lie—when they learn that they do not have to tell what is in their heart, when they tell their mothers that they don't have a cookie when they're really hiding one behind their back—they gain a certain autonomy.

One of the definitions of an autistic disorder—so I gather, I'm not a serious student of this—involves the inability to do just that. Autistic kids have problems knowing when someone else is lying, they have problems in distinguishing between their own internal reality and what they can say. This is one of the problems, I understand, that apparently defines autism.

To think otherwise, then, we might say, is a very human capacity. Lying has this almost utopian side to it. And Hannah Arendt, in particular, points this out.

HB: But I think that this utopian side of lying is often unappreciated in the public consciousness, certainly in a society in which people are castigating certain individuals for lying.

We mentioned this earlier in our discussion of Christopher Hitchens and his earlier statements that lying is the sine qua non of immoral political behaviour. I think this notion that lying isn't necessarily always a bad thing is an important one to convey.

Did that resonate with people in terms of their response to this book? Did they pick up on that?

MJ: The response was mixed, as I expected it to be. There are people who still hold to a very strong moralistic attitude whereby lying is problematic in general in politics, where there is supposed to be trust.

HB: Sure. But you are not advocating breaking public trust.

MJ: No. It's a funny ideal. As I said earlier, trust in **what**? In doing what's best for *everyone*? In telling the truth *no matter what*? We trust in various things—in God we trust, even if we don't believe in God.

There's a kind of funny way in which there's an *"I-know-but-I don't-know"* quality in that. I think the crucial thing is to think of the wariness that we have about lying as something that we can't give up. We ought not to be completely cynical about it. My book is one that argues against the notion that politics is just the realm of self-interest, of corruption, of cynicism. It urges that something good gets done, even when people suspend overly moral, regulative ideals. Some people got that.

And then there are a number of other books that I cite by people who take seriously the positive functions, under certain circumstances, of lying.

With respect to the notion of utopian hopes I was speaking about a moment ago, there's a wonderful book by Jean-Michel Rabaté (*The Ethics of the Lie*) on the idea of *le mensonge*, in which the notion of *songe*, or "dream," in *mensonge* is taken seriously: you're dreaming of something else. So there's that aspect to it as well.

And I think we had, with the Snowden revelations, a very interesting example of the potential dysfunction of an overly truth-telling situation. It was a situation where *everything* was disclosed and peoples' lives—those of spies, in particular—were put in jeopardy, people were embarrassed. Was it in the service of better politics? I'm not so sure.

There are people, like Daniel Ellsberg, who will say that it was, that everything should be disclosed, that corruption and malfeasance should always be revealed, and so forth. Well, of course, the Snowden affair was only one-sided: we saw what our government did, but we didn't see what other governments were doing. There's a difference between everyone being outed and only some people being outed.

Questions for Discussion:

1. What would the effects of a perfectly functioning polygraph test have on international and domestic politics?

2. To what extent is our ability to lie fundamentally related to notions of free will and responsibility?

VI. Monological Dangers
Truth as the enemy of the political

HB: I think most people understand the whole idea of a white lie. In French, as you pointed out in your book, there is this intriguing notion of, literally, *"a pious lie"*—occasions when people can, and maybe even *should*, lie. There are extreme versions of this—the *Inglourious Basterds* scenario, "the murderer-at-the-door", that you mentioned earlier—but even on a day-to-day level we all know that we shouldn't tell people they look horrible, even if they do.

MJ: Exactly. This is the socialization of politeness. A society in which politeness is overly valued is a society in which everything is superficial. The classic example is the court of Louis XIV followed by the Puritans' response—Pascal and other Jansenists against the Jesuits and so forth.

So there are lots of ways in which we understand how politeness can be taken too far. But without politeness—without a sense of civility, without a sense of sparing the feelings of the other person, without a sense of smoothing over potential adversarial relationships—society wouldn't function. Sociologists like Georg Simmel noted that.

Now, white lies are usually pretty innocuous, but this is where the religious debates are interesting. If, say, in a Protestant country during the sixteenth century, you admit to being Catholic, then you can be killed

The Church then says, *"All right, we don't want you killed. You have a pass to make a mental reservation."* There's also the Islamic notion of *taqiyya*, which is essentially the same thing. There are various ways in which even those seemingly rigorous moral-cum-religious systems understand circumstantially that there are moments when one has to be relatively disingenuous.

HB: There's a higher prioritization: since your survival is a higher priority, then you have to give more weight to that.

MJ: The other way to think about it is as competing moral commands. I may lie to help someone else: I may lie not for my own survival, but for somebody else's survival.

One of the people who deals with this sort of complexity is Rousseau, when he says, *"Look, lying serves your self-interest."* And, of course, in the case of someone who is accused of being a Catholic in a Protestant country, it *is* self-interest, but you get a pass on that.

But if it is *just* for your self-interest—for instance, if you're lying just to gain an advantage in a commercial transaction—then that's not so good. If you lie for the benefit of somebody else—if you jeopardize your soul for the benefit of somebody else—that has a nobler potential.

The issue—and again, this is where Kant, I think, is problematic—is not so much that there is a hierarchy of moral commands and we always know which ones to follow, but rather the fact that very often in a complex world there are many different moral commands, many different pragmatic imperatives, many different reasons for why we act. We don't act out of impulse itself, but with real reasons.

We may have a moral debate within ourselves before we choose to lie or be hypocritical, or we may decide that we must tell the truth no matter what the circumstances, or we may decide that we have other concerns that we take seriously as countervailing reasons not to lie.

HB: So, you can't just have these inflexible, universal moral laws that pertain to whatever the situation may be at all times and in all instances. You have to use judgment; you have to recognize the countervailing factors that are in play.

And interestingly, again, this has a concrete manifestation in the political realm, and leads you to the conclusion that lying may not always be such a bad thing. If you were to tell the average person on the street this, she'd likely deny it outright. But if she'd think about it, she might come to that very same conclusion.

MJ: The deeper reason why I think that's the case—and this is an Arendtian argument; Hannah Arendt made this very clear—is because truth is, in a way, the enemy of the political.

That is to say, truth is singular and monological: there is a truth, and everything else is a falsehood or an error. Therefore, there are certain discursive contexts in which we aim for the truth.

Science, for instance, tries to come up with the truth. Sometimes, in a juridical situation, we try to come up with the truth about whether or not a person committed a crime. We understand that, in those cases, the telos of the discourse is truth-telling.

In politics, there are opinions, and there are countervailing interests. In politics, we are projecting ourselves into a future that is not yet capable of being amenable to the truth: we don't know the truth about the future.

Politics is a game in which the truth is perhaps a dangerous goal, because it's so singular. As I point out in the book, "the big truth" is, in a way, the mirror image of "the big lie", in that we try to create a heterocosm—a new universe—which is perfectly consistent, in which everything fits, in which there is a kind of pseudo-truth—which is, in fact a lie. It's like *The Truman Show*, where you live in a bubble.

What we need instead, it seems to me, is an awareness of the fact that we have lots of little, if not full lies, half-truths, spins, opinions—a plurality of different positions, which never congeal into a single, monological truth that is then represented by a single party or a single figure; or anything that leads to a kind of totalitarian notion that the truth is embodied in one political institution or person.

Instead, we understand politics as precisely the realm of contingency: of openness and plurality, of something that allows humility, allows for the idea that we are fallible, that we may not get it right.

Politics is often filled with unintended consequences, and therefore we can't really have, ever, a monopoly on the truth. If we have any definition of totalitarianism, it is precisely the attempt to create that one single truth with a single and totally monopolistic notion of what politics should be.

This is why I talk about the "aesthetic moment" in politics and Ernst Kantorowicz's remarkably rich use of the notion of the "King's Two Bodies."

Even in a democracy, we get the distinction between the *ideal body* of "the people"—a populous sovereignty, which is like the *corpus mysticum*, the mystical body of Christ, or like the king's royal body, which exists even when the king dies—and the *real people*—you and me who are actually voting for some particular party that claims to represent "the people", in other words, the actual population in question.

"The people" itself, is a contested term, and it should always remain contested. It should always remain at a distance from, and never be conflated with, the *real people* involved.

Lying is, in a way, built into that, because we often speak in the name of "the people," but in fact "the people" is always this kind of will-o'-the-wisp, something we never quite reach even though in some systems there is a collapse between "the people" and its institutions, which is dangerous.

Questions for Discussion:

1. Should "white lies" really be called "lies" at all?

2. To what extent can we ever objectively assess to what extent a successful politician has a "mandate from the people"?

VII. Democracy
Its porous nature and implications

HB: How much, in your judgment, are these ideas, these arguments, necessarily tied to the democratic project? Is there a sense that they are necessarily relevant to democracy, and perhaps much more irrelevant to any other form of government, like oligarchy, quasi-representational government, monarchy, what have you?

MJ: First of all, a democracy is itself an enormously complicated notion. We are not sure what it means; it's not something that has ever really been achieved. It's a kind of desideratum.

HB: Sure. You've got classical, Athenian democracy on the one hand, which is very different from virtually any form of democracy today.

MJ: And, of course, the Athenians left women and slaves out, so they too were not the perfect democracy. We know that democracy is an ideal, and that democratization is a process, and that this process is always in danger of being undermined. It's not as if we live in a static thing called "democracy."

The other thing to say about democracy is that it is always porous, in the sense that there are other institutions—such as, for example, a free press—which can do muckraking journalism and try to uncover the truth, try to test lies. We need that. Democracy does not simply involve "the political arena", but is also in play with other arenas.

Even science—which, as I said earlier, has a kind-of monological, truth-telling orientation—intersects with democracy, so that we get information from science, such as in formation about climate change. We take science seriously, or at least we should, even though people play politics with it. We take the lessons of experts. So politics is not just you and me deciding by a vote whether or not there is actually climate change; we take seriously what experts say.

In other words, politics—and democracy in general—is porous and open: it's not fully contained. But within that relatively porous container—the democratic realm of decision-making—there are, I think, always adversarial as well as collaborative relationships.

The adversarial relationships, as I said earlier, often involve a kind-of strategic use of lying. But even in collaborative relationships in democracy—even in building coalitions—there is a space for a kind of forgetting of differences, in which we create, say, for a particular election, an alliance between this wing of my party and the other wing of the party, in which I forget that there are real differences between them.

The great example we have in international relations, which I provide in the book, concerns the allies in World War II. Hitler is the enemy, and the Japanese are the enemy. The alliance between Stalin, Churchill, and Roosevelt is an alliance of people who are basically fudging the fact that they disagree over many fundamental things: communism versus capitalism; British imperialism versus the attempt to decolonize.

This was based on a kind of, if not lying, let us say "suspension of the truth". The Cold War breaks out immediately after the Second World War is won, so the conflict was always there, latent. But this is what happens in coalitions. Democracy works through coalitions in which one suspends truth-telling.

For another instance, consider a primary election, where you have people who are at each other's throats for a prolonged period of time. Each of them will say that the other guy is a total scoundrel, a fool, and so on. But after one person wins, suddenly the party rallies around him; and before you know it, one of the guys who was attacking him in the primary becomes the party's vice-presidential candidate. We all know that's the way it works. Democracy needs, we might say, the lubrication of a certain suspension of absolute truth-telling.

There are also people who go into politics and cry, "*I'm trying to get elected,*" even though they know they have no chance of being elected—no chance whatsoever. Yet, they go in, because they want to have their ideas heard, they want to shake the system up, they want to start a third party. But we know, and they know, and everybody knows, that they have no chance.

HB: And they will never say that publicly.

MJ: They *can't* say it. It's part of the decorum of the political, to fabulate. And, then, occasionally, something happens that no one expects. So politics—once again, because it is future-oriented—is a place in which the fib can become the truth.

Questions for Discussion:

1. On the whole, do you think that democracies are liable to produce more, less, or the same amount of lies than other political systems?

2. To what extent do our political systems assume a collective lack of memory—or interest—of what was said from one month to the next?

VIII. Getting Worse?

In search of a Golden Age of truth-telling

HB: Suppose that I'm some guy on the street somewhere who generally agrees with what you've been saying. I understand that there is not this absolute, strict, Kantian rule of morality which applies universally to all times and places. I understand, too, that part of leadership might necessarily entail not always telling the truth.

"*But*," I maintain, "*there's something different going on today, because it's not just that politicians are promising one thing and not delivering, or that they're just telling a lie here or there. No, now there's this deliberate misrepresentation of what others have actually said, so that you can't even get to the point of beginning any critical discourse. There's this massive misportrayal of what some people have said or done, or of basic historical events, which prohibits any sort of meaningful dialogue and exchange.*"

The argument is that we have now reached a point that we are lying—we are deliberately and wilfully misrepresenting things—to a degree that far surpasses what has occurred in the past, and which might prohibit us from actually having a fully functional democracy in the future.

MJ: You often hear this: things are getting worse.

During the George W. Bush presidency, for instance, there was a great deal of that kind of rhetoric concerning weapons of mass destruction, as well as many other things. There was a flood of books during that time, both on the right and the left, about lying.

The kind of research that I did in a way helps to defuse that narrative, because it shows that at many other moments in history there have also been panics about lying: worries that politicians are nothing but scoundrels, sentiments that, in the words of I.F. Stone, "all governments lie,"—an awareness that people are being lied to and that politicians are lying about what other people are saying.

This is such a constant refrain that the idea that things are just getting worse *also* becomes a constant refrain. People come to believe that there was a "Golden Age"—a period when giants walked the earth and everyone was Gandhi.

Of course that isn't true. Throughout American history, and through other historical eras, there is an unbelievable amount of bad faith: it's far more frequent than one imagines. We always think that we're living in a period of decline and that there was once a period of plain-speaking. That is not true.

The other issue is, of course, the fact that we now have a much more rapid response to lying, with the media and the Internet: people don't get away with it as much. I can't misrepresent what my opponent said if he has a tape indicating exactly what he said, and vice-versa. There are various ways in which we can quickly uncover falsehoods and force people to own up to them.

I think we now have both a proliferation of lies, spread through the media, and also the ability to very quickly respond to and defuse the spread of a rumour. But certainly, rumours, which are another example of a kind of lie, have occurred in the past in ways that are remarkably prevalent in almost any context.

HB: Are the media today doing a sufficiently good job, in terms of holding politicians accountable, being responsive, and distinguishing between "important" lies and "unimportant" lies?

MJ: Well, I'm also not a serious student of the media, but I would also say that there is an alarm out there that the patience to do serious investigative journalism is wearing thin and the money sponsoring this sort of journalism is not as forthcoming as it once was.

We now have sound-bite journalism for shorter attention spans—people don't read long articles. But every so often a longer piece will occur—in *The New York Times* or *The New Yorker* or *The Huffington*

Post—where somebody will have spent a lot of time investigating, and in which things *do* come out.

I would also say that there is a premium placed on the "scoop," on showing that some politician has done something really problematic.

Now, there is probably a lot of stuff that we *don't* get to see: we don't really know if more terrible things are happening, we don't know that which journalism fails to alert us to.

I think journalists—and I have great respect for serious journalists—are doing the best they can with limited resources and with the monopolization of media, which is always an issue—the control that people like Rupert Murdoch have. But on the whole I think there are people doing very credible things to expose political chicanery.

Questions for Discussion:

1. What do you think Martin means by "the monopolization of the media"? To what extent is this a problem?

2. Do politicians lie more today than they used to? If so, how can we be certain that that's the case? If not, why do you think so many people seem convinced that this is happening?

3. Is "fake news" a recent phenomenon? Is it even an actual phenomenon?

IX. Puritanical Dangers
Fanatical truth-telling

HB: I'd like to briefly return to this idea of the American-style truth-teller: George Washington, the cherry tree and the straight-talking fellow who is cutting through all the lies and superficiality and reinventing the world to the good.

Is there a sense, through your reading and your research, that there are societies that have a greater tolerance—a greater understanding, a greater amount of sophistication, if you will—toward the necessity, or the inevitability, of lying in the public sphere? Is America different in this respect? Or is it fairly the same across the board?

MJ: I think, historically, there have been moments in which people understood that a certain amount of semblance, a certain amount of deception, is part of the social fabric. It's like corruption: in some societies corruption is endemic. We can be moralistic about it, but it functions, in some way—maybe badly, but it does function.

There are other societies where there is a kind of purism: the Protestant Reformation is a good example of this. In this case, there was a widespread impatience with the indulgences of the Church, which was generally considered too self-absorbed and hypocritical about saving souls rather than living well. There are historical moments when there is a kind of purification campaign.

Sometimes this can have pretty awful consequences. Take ISIS today, this very frightening movement, a movement for a kind of purification, a movement for truth-telling. They show you videos of the horrors they commit. They're not hypocritical: they behead people and they proudly show you the beheadings.

To the extent that we can make sense of what they are doing, they are a purification movement. They are very clear about purifying their own society of infidels, including other Muslims who don't conform to their version of Islam. And they're also, in a way, truth-telling, because they are focused on using the media to explicitly show what they do: the atrocities, the horrors, the beheadings.

HB: They're proudly truth-telling.

MJ: They are "in-your-face" truth-telling, in the same way that many people would say that Hitler was not trying to dissemble, but told you what he was going to do and did it.

Another great example of this is Robespierre, who was famously against hypocrisy and corruption—he called himself "The Incorruptible". And The Terror—to the extent that we understand The Terror as being derived from his ideas—was a result of that.

Purity, truth-telling, incorruptibility, absoluteness—all of these can lead to rather coercive effects. It comes back to the idea of the truth in politics being of less value than it is, perhaps, in other realms. We should live with fallibility, live with our own inability to know "the Truth with a capital T".

Questions for Discussion:

1. To what extent is the core danger highlighted in this chapter more a question of bragging about truth-telling—sanctimoniousness—rather than truth-telling per se?

2. What do you think Martin means, exactly, when he says that in some societies endemic corruption does "function, in a way"?

X. Politics vs. Science
Similarities and differences

HB: I think this relates to what you were saying before about the mistake that Kant made: his advocating the imposition of a law-like regularity on human behaviour and morals.

Recently, I talked to your UC Berkeley colleague Mark Bevir (*How Social Science Creates the World*), who has very strong views about the necessary historical contingency of politics. He's strongly opposed to the idea of irrevocable, unbreakable universal laws of human behaviour, believing that politics is an art of interpretation, a necessarily grey area that is an essential aspect of the human condition.

But this leads me to another point from a somewhat different perspective. You've talked about this idea of "leakage" from the political sphere to other spheres, and I'd like to talk now about politics vis-à-vis science.

Most scientists believe that there is a collective effort towards converging upon the truth. We've talked about the danger of looking at politics from that perspective: that it's naive, and in fact could have all sorts of negative repercussions. But often the leakage seems to go the other way.

Here's what I mean to say. Journalists who cover politics will say, for example, "*We understand that people lie and dissemble, which is an inevitable part of politics: there are always two sides to every story. If I hear some Republican say something, I know that he is saying it with an agenda, and it's exactly the same thing for a Democrat. There is no objective truth out there.*"

This drives scientists completely crazy, because the assumption is that we can apply this mentality to other areas of inquiry, namely science. But for a scientist, that is just *not* the way it is: there *aren't* always two sides to every story—or at least two sides worth being listened to.

Personally, I think this way of thinking can really be pernicious, because it represents a lack of understanding of the fact that these domains are very separate, and that there should be *less* leakage than there is. Does that resonate with you in any way?

MJ: It's a complicated issue, because, obviously, some interpenetration occurs in ways that make us wisely accept the counsel of science. I mentioned climate change as one such instance of this.

HB: Well, there's science as public policy, and then there's science as science. There's a difference.

MJ: That's also another interesting way to think about it: "*Should we have moral issues with stem cell research or not?*" is different from "*Would stem cell research allow us to solve medical problems?*" There are two levels.

On the issue of whether or not science simplifies the truth and is monological: its telos—its goal—is that, but in fact science often operates through a dialectic of different positions where people argue. And sometimes science is unsettled, sometimes what we thought was the truth turns out to be false.

Even scientists who have great confidence in what they're doing, if they're aware of the history of science, will know that people in the past also had confidence and got it wrong—think of eugenics, or other things that were once "good science" that we are now very, very nervous about. So even science is open to dispute.

Having said that, the protocols of the scientific method and the scientific community—the procedures of peer-review and replication, and so forth—much as they are under pressure, are nonetheless more on the side of looking for a kind of disinterested truth. Scientists may get personal feelings of esteem from, say, winning a Nobel Prize, but they are nonetheless interested in figuring out a problem.

Whereas in politics there is always interest, there is always opinion. So there is a kind of tension between science and politics, but also a kind of dialogue. The worst thing would be to create a model of politics in the image of science, in which there is an elite of people who have the tools, the background, the training and the credentials to tell us what to do.

In the 1920s, Walter Lippmann thought this was the way we should go: a kind of technocratic politics in which only the people who really know should somehow help the rest of us figure out what we should do.

Jürgen Habermas, who was a great inspiration in many respects for my work—and who is not a believer, incidentally, I would say, in the virtues of lying—argues that in the process of enlightenment we are all participants: there is no elite which tutors the rest of us, there is no expert group that can tell us what we should do.

I think this is crucial about science. Scientists put on two different caps. When they enter the political realm—and there are politically-oriented scientists, like Linus Pauling and others, who have tried to argue for certain positions—they have to recognize that they are participants in the debate: they bring their expertise, but we as non-scientists bring our own interests and judgments as well.

It's a dialogue, rather than one group dominating the other. I think scientists are wrong if they get impatient with politics because it's messy. They ought to understand what politics is, and not see it in the model of science.

HB: I certainly agree with that. My point is that there are two things going on, as you pointed out. On the one hand, there is science itself, and the public perception of what the scientific practice is: an objective convergence upon some sense of truth. I think that this perception is largely correct. I think that if you look around you, in the age in which we live, you find that what separates us from a multitude of other civilizations and societies is our awareness and our harnessing of objective scientific truths. I certainly don't think this is true in all respects, but I think that, as a general rule of thumb, there's a lot to be said for it.

On the other hand, science is an activity that is being practiced by human beings, which means that scientists are subject to the same distortions and megalomania and clan mentality that other humans are. I think, too, that one has to distinguish between the process and the outcomes, which deserve to be regarded on their own merits, and the individuals who are lobbying for this or that.

And what's interesting to me is that there is also this public sphere concerned with implementing the findings of science, of linking scientific knowledge with public policy.

I suppose what I'm arguing is that it's important to recognize that a scientific consensus is different from a political consensus. It's a horse of a different colour. It doesn't mean that it is necessarily the truth—as you say, often people go down the wrong road and the consensus today may not be the consensus tomorrow—but it has a much higher likelihood, in my view, than most other areas.

MJ: I think it's a sort of truth discourse, in which the goal is to somehow suspend one's own private interests, opinions, values, and background in order to have a kind of collective subject, the scientific community, develop through its supposedly disinterested vetting processes—blind peer-review, verification through replication, all of that—a different outcome from political experiment.

There is, though, on a meta-level, a very interesting issue of whether or not always telling the truth, always seeking the truth, is necessarily in the service of humankind.

The great example of this is the unleashing of atomic energy. Of course, some of the scientists who worked on the Manhattan Project had second thoughts afterwards. Should they have gone down that route? Was this simply seeking the truth, or was it a pact with the devil?

So there are some ways in which we make decisions about which science we support, which science—which truth-telling—we try to pursue. And a lot of this is a question of scarce resources: How much money can we give to this project? How much money can we give to another project? Should we try to land on Mars, or should we try to cure cancer? There are lots of issues in which truth-telling is already embedded in other human concerns.

But I agree that there is an interesting tension between politics and science, and I think that is a good thing. Once again there is the issue of the boundary, or lack thereof, between the political and other realms. Politics is in relation to other things, and sometimes those other things are politicized. Who gets the Nobel Prize in physics may not be a fully scientific question.

HB: But that's not science.

MJ: It's not science, but it also involves funding and other things—

HB: But that's not science, either.

MJ: But we have this ideal of science, just as we do the "pure political". Science is always both a disinterested pursuit and what historians and sociologists of science tell us it really is, which may be certain credentialed people operating in certain not-so disinterested ways.

Again, there's this mixture of the ideal and the real. I wouldn't say that we should collapse one into the other—we shouldn't go either down or up—but science is different from the way the political operates, and yet they're interpenetrated. It's more complex than any single rule of thumb. The interpenetration exists, but without the collapse.

Questions for Discussion:

1. Do you agree or disagree with Howard that "a scientific consensus is different than a political consensus"?

2. Under what circumstances can we make a clear distinction between scientific knowledge and how it could or should be used?

XI. Summing Up
Admissions and conclusions

HB: Let me sum up with a question about your awareness of, not so much lying, but the political project, through the course of this research. Have you been surprised by things? Have you developed a deeper understanding about some things? Has this enabled you to look at some of these more profound sociological or philosophical issues from a different perspective?

MJ: Well, I think something like this alerted me to things I intuited before, which is that there is no single normative notion of politics.

In the 1960s—I grew up in the 1960s—there was a sense of the expansion of politics: the personal as the political, politics from below, politics in the streets, politics outside of representative democracy, politics outside of parties—politics that somehow had an impact on the system but didn't fully overthrow, or change, or revolutionize the system. So politics expands, it contracts, it has no simple understanding of what it does. Democracy is always en route.

I was also fascinated by the way in which the attempt to isolate the political—by Carl Schmitt, Hannah Arendt, and others—has its virtues, but also its limits.

We can understand the political as being relatively—but not absolutely—autonomous, in relation to other human endeavours, such as science or religion or morality or economics or other subsystems of the whole that have *their* relative autonomy.

In complex, differentiated societies, then, the political has its own momentum, its own institutions, its own protocols, its own internal dynamic; and yet it is also in conversation with, penetrated by, and sometimes beholden to, other dimensions of the world.

This is ongoing: there's no final formula.

I was very interested in the complexities of the moral issues that this kind of research raised. Things are not always as simple as you assumed at the beginning of the game. This is not to say that you are paralyzed and can't operate because you end up with so much complexity that everything is a bad alternative, but it does give you some sense of how difficult it is to be certain about the choices you made.

HB: Were you surprised by anything?

MJ: Was I surprised? I suppose I didn't fully anticipate having to parse the various versions of the political when I began.

I thought I already more or less knew what politics is, but it turned out that I had to do much more digging into the various versions of the political, and even then I only scratched the surface. That was kind of fun.

Before you talk about lying and politics, you have to really understand what all these various versions of politics—democratic, international, domestic, adversarial, collaborative—entail, and how they then interface with questions about lying. It becomes a series of moving targets rather than a single fixed one. That was exciting. I like both complexity and the ability to make some sense of it—without, I hope, reducing it to its simplest dimensions.

HB: Right.

Although *you're* not interested in reducing things to their simplest dimensions, and *I'm* not interested in reducing things to their simplest dimensions, nonetheless if you *had* to reduce things to their simplest dimensions and give a brief encapsulation for the average person of what you think we should take away from this whole discussion of lying and politics, what would you say?

MJ: I think the one lesson that comes out of this is to be more attentive to the substantive issues, and less concerned with the character and truth-telling—self-pretensions, we might say—of the person who is defending them.

Sometimes scoundrels produce good outcomes, and sometimes pious, well-intentioned people produce lousy outcomes. One has to be aware of the fact that the person who beats his chest and says, "*I am the truth-teller. I am authentic. The other guy is the liar,*" may be basically leading us down a garden path. This is not to say that character counts for nothing, but we shouldn't vote for saints. We should vote for people who will produce outcomes that are beneficial. That is more important: substance over style.

I don't think this is cynical. I think it's an awareness of how politics works for us, how it lubricates a system in which there is no single truth and in which character is *part* of the equation, but not the *entire* equation.

HB: That doesn't sound cynical at all to me. But it does sound dangerously verificationist. It seems like you're moving toward a science, after all.

MJ: Well, it's pragmatist, in a broad sense. I'm interested in outcomes, and unintended consequences are the name of the game. One has to be aware of intentions and take them seriously—we have them ourselves, we hope for good outcomes—but also be sensitive to the context and the complexities of where those intentions might lead.

Which means that we shouldn't always follow the alleged "authentic" politician, who tells us what his character is like and explains everything from his own good heart while basically demonizing the others: the phony, the liar, the hypocrite, the scoundrel.

HB: Is there anything I didn't ask—anything else you'd like to comment on?

MJ: No, we covered a lot of territory. That was fun. Thanks.

HB: Thanks a lot, Martin. That was great.

Questions for Discussion:

1. To what extent do you think "the political" can be meaningfully identified and distinguished from other domains?

2. Has this conversation changed your perspective of the lying in politics today? If so, in what way, exactly?

Continuing the Conversation

Readers are encouraged to read Martin's book, *The Virtues of Mendacity: On Lying in Politics*, which goes into considerable additional detail about many of the issues discussed here.

Those with an interest in the Frankfurt School are referred to his books, *Splinters in Your Eye: Essays on the Frankfurt School* and *The Dialectical Imagination: A History of the Frankfurt School and the Institute of Social Research, 1923–1950*.

Quest for Freedom

A conversation with Quentin Skinner

Introduction
Status Symbols

What does it mean to be free?

That hardly seems like a terribly difficult question to answer. I'm free if I'm unconstrained, unimpeded, allowed to act as I see fit. Simple, right?

Well, maybe.

Quentin Skinner, one of the world's foremost intellectual historians, admits that the concept of freedom had long befuddled him.

> *"It began with historical work that I was doing when I was writing my first book,* **The Foundations of Modern Political Thought**. *I was working on questions about Renaissance moral and political philosophy and came upon some ideas that, quite frankly, puzzled me, because I was assuming that there would be great continuity in thinking about questions of freedom and citizenship, but there wasn't. I was coming upon a view that suggested that you could not be a free citizen unless you were a politically engaged citizen."*

It's not difficult to see the problem. For most of us, being politically active simply has nothing to do with our sense of being free.

In his customarily forthright fashion, Quentin shared with me his intellectual meanderings. Could it be that what he was grappling with was simply a rehashed view of Aristotle's famous dictum that man was a political animal? That, as a naturally political creature, the free man was the exemplar of the species, the one who best realized his potential and thus was somehow maximally political?

That freedom in some way represented some sort of acme of human moral potential?

Perhaps. After all, he admits, there was a good deal of modern precedent for such neo-Aristotelian thinking. The renowned 20th-century philosopher Hannah Arendt, in particular, makes an essential equivalence between freedom and politics.

> *"For her, freedom just **is** politics. That is to say, the democratic project of people being thoroughly engaged as citizens is an instantiation and a declaration of freedom. So I started to think that **that** was what I was confronting."*

But still, things didn't quite fit. He couldn't help feeling that the proper way to look at things wasn't so much a description of human potential, but rather a societal prescription for ensuring that you don't lose what you've already got. In other words, as Quentin puts it:

> *"The more I read, the more I saw that the claim that was being made was a **causal** claim. In a way, that seemed more intuitive when I thought about it. The claim seemed to be that if you want to remain free as a citizen, then it's a causal condition of the maintenance of that freedom that you should actively participate in the life of your community."*

This, Quentin recognized, was a very different kettle of fish than the notion of the free person being unencumbered to perform this or that action. While the word—"freedom"—was clearly the same, writers in the Renaissance and Ancient Rome were actually using it in an entirely different way.

> *"What the writers I was finding in the Renaissance, and then back to Roman—as opposed to Greek—antiquity wanted to say, is that freedom should not be understood as a predicate of actions, essentially, **at all**. Freedom is the name of a **status**. That's what they wanted us to understand. Their emphasis was not on whether I'm free to do this or that. Of course that was important to them. But what was*

*fundamental to them was the question, **Do you have the status of being a free person?** That's the question they're asking."*

So score one for Professor Skinner's literary detective skills. But why should we care whether or not classical Romans or Renaissance thinkers used terms like "freedom" differently from the way we do now? Isn't that just all ancient history?

No. Because Quentin believes truly understanding these classical thinkers might significantly inform our judgements as we grapple with some of today's pressing issues. When governments spy on our emails, for instance, they don't just violate our privacy (although they surely do that as well), they cause us—ever so slightly—to think differently, to act differently. We begin to consider leaving things out of our correspondence that could conceivably be regarded as incriminating. We begin to write different sorts of messages altogether—perhaps don't bother to write them at all. In other words, we start censoring ourselves.

To an ancient Roman, such behaviour could be categorized quite simply: we start acting "slavishly", rather than as free men.

> "Nobody is stopping me, no one is interfering directly with me writing the emails I want to write. But again, that's the way of thinking about freedom superficially. That's surface stuff.
>
> "What we're talking about is something much more fundamental, a democratic citizen thinking, **Well, I don't know if I can really say this anymore.** And that's the point: I **don't know**. That's what it is to live like a slave in a certain domain: you don't know what might happen to you."

And if "never knowing what might happen to you" is the lot of the slave, how can the free citizen guarantee that this never happens to her—that her free status is protected? By ensuring that she lives in a society with no arbitrary powers beyond her control—by ensuring that the rule of law applies in all circumstances, and that the law itself is a clear expression of the free citizen's will.

> *"What this mandates is a particular form of a very active democratic citizenship as a condition of upholding freedom, but not as a condition of upholding freedom as being left alone to do whatever I want. The freedom that is being upheld is **freedom from arbitrary power**, because if you're not free from arbitrary power, you don't have freedom in this absolutely fundamental sense."*

We've arrived, then, at the claim that safeguarding our civil liberties and protecting ourselves from the encroachment of arbitrary powers requires an active participation in the democratic process.

Somehow, from ruminating on the precise motivations of celebrated Renaissance thinkers, we're led to a core belief about the importance of civic action that you could easily imagine hearing at any *Black Lives Matter* protest.

If that's not a palpable demonstration of the ongoing relevance of the history of ideas, I'm not sure what is.

The Conversation

I. Paradoxical Origins
Puzzled by Machiavelli

HB: Let me begin by asking you a personal question about liberty and your interest in political liberty. How did that begin for you?

QS: It began with historical work that I was doing when I was writing my first book, *The Foundations of Modern Political Thought*. I was working on questions about Renaissance moral and political philosophy and came upon some ideas that, quite frankly, puzzled me, because I was assuming that there would be great continuity in thinking about questions of freedom and citizenship, but there wasn't. I was coming upon a view that suggested that you could not be a free citizen unless you were a politically engaged citizen.

Something was being strongly affirmed, especially in a writer like Machiavelli in the *Discourses on Livy*, which seemed the opposite of what our intuitions would be, which is that freedom should be thought of mainly in terms of *rights*. And fundamental rights include rights to be left alone, so far as is compatible with a good legal order, and getting along with one's life in the way that one chooses. The notion that freedom would involve *action*—which would not be strongly chosen action, but would be almost obligatory—was a paradox that I came upon and couldn't, at that time, properly resolve.

HB: When you first saw this, did it make you immediately think of the ideology of Roman times? Did you think of Cicero and his sense that it's the duty of any high-born, or at least sufficiently capable, free citizen of Rome to be participating in the welfare of his state? Did that come to your mind immediately, or did it take a little bit longer? Or did it not come that way at all?

QS: It *should* have come that way, and I certainly looked to antiquity because the people in the Renaissance were all looking to antiquity, but I looked in the wrong place. What I thought I was bound to be driven back to was an Aristotelian understanding of citizenship, in which, to paraphrase very strongly, Aristotle wants us to suppose that human nature has an essence. I suppose we don't completely disagree with that: we talk about actions as inhuman and so forth. But this human essence, for Aristotle, was political. As he says in the famous phrase, "*Man is the political animal.*"

I thought that what I was reading was a revival of this idea that there is a kind of essence to human nature, that the essence is political, and then the strong claim—which is almost on the edge of sense—that what it is to be a free person, especially what it is to be a citizen, is to realize those capacities, to realize those particular powers, because those are your distinctively human powers.

HB: To maximize the potentiality of what it means to be human, according to this definition.

QS: Yes, exactly. So freedom comes to be seen as the name of a kind of moral achievement where you have it in you to become something, and the free person is the person who realizes those potentialities. That's recognizably a Greek way of thinking about the relationship of potentiality to power. Of course, that's also a view of freedom that is at large in our own day—and I think that must have helped me to go on the wrong track.

When I was growing up, the philosopher who above all had made that her view about freedom was Hannah Arendt, especially in the essays in *Between Past and Future* when she talks about freedom and politics. For her, freedom just *is* politics—that is to say, the democratic project of people being thoroughly engaged as citizens is an instantiation and a declaration of freedom. So I started to think that this was what I was confronting.

But the more I read, the more I saw that the claim that was being made was a *causal* claim. In a way, that seemed more intuitive when I thought about it. The claim seemed to be that if you want to remain free as a citizen, then it's a causal condition of the maintenance of that freedom that you should actively participate in the life of your community.

HB: Of course, that's not such an unusual thing for Machiavelli to be saying, given his circumstances.

QS: That's right. It's a view about the relationship of freedom to self-government.

The second phase in my interest in these questions arose when I was invited to give something called *The Tanner Lectures* at Harvard University. This was very shortly after I published my first book, which came out in 1978, so I must have been asked to give these lectures sometime in the very early 1980s. I delivered them in 1984. I gave a series of lectures called *The Paradoxes of Political Liberty*, in which I offered this kind of Stoic paradox that freedom was seen as service. I tried to work through the causal account of that which I'd arrived at, but I wasn't very satisfied with it. I didn't think it was wrong, but it had left me feeling that I hadn't really understood what the underlying view of freedom was.

Then I went on to other phases of my research, and I didn't come back to this question until sometime later when I was working again on Renaissance thought. That was in the early 1990s. I had a great stroke of luck at that time: I was at the Australian National University on a research fellowship, and an old friend of mine, Philip Pettit, who now teaches at Princeton University, was then in the Research School of Social Sciences and was working on questions about freedom. He and I taught a seminar together. I think it was Philip who had the insight that I had been casting around for sometime before, which was that what makes sense of all of these things that I've said so far is that when these republican writers of the Renaissance and early modern period talk about freedom, they just don't mean anything like how we would understand the concept.

As a historian, I should have been having that insight. I could see that it wasn't fitting together. But Philip supplied a version of what I've come to think is fundamental to this, as I want to call it, *neo-Roman* way of thinking about freedom, which was to say that, for us, the natural way of thinking about political liberty and civil freedom of any kind, is to think of it as *de facto*.

That is to say, *Are you now free to do something or refrain from doing it?* is simply a question about whether anyone else is interfering with your exercise of your powers. It's de facto in the sense that if no one is stopping you from doing something, if you have the power to do that thing and you choose to do it, that's a free choice. And the resulting action is a free action.

That's a very natural way for us to think about freedom. In fact, it's the standard way we think about freedom. But the writers I was studying were not thinking about freedom in that way at all.

Philip Pettit wrote a brilliant, now classic, book, published in 1997—the same year that I published *Liberty before Liberalism*—called *Republicanism: A Theory of Freedom and Government*, in which he proposed a view that wasn't quite the view that I eventually wanted to put forward, but helped me tremendously to go on my way. This was the view that we should distinguish freedom understood as non-interference, as he wanted to call it, from freedom understood as non-domination.

He wanted a very strong symmetry between two different ways of thinking about negative liberty. These are both ways of thinking about liberty as a *negative* concept—by which I mean that the presence of freedom is always recognizable by an absence.

The liberal understanding of freedom is that the absence that always marks the presence of freedom is absence of interference; whereas the presence that marks the absence of liberty in what he calls republican terms, would be the presence of domination.

Now, I appreciate, because Philip is a philosopher rather than an intellectual historian, that he liked this symmetry very much, and he wanted to bring the two stories strongly together, while contrasting them.

It seemed to me, as I was writing about this issue at the same time in *Liberty before Liberalism*, that the contrast was actually dramatically much wider than that formulation might lead one to think. What the writers I was finding in the Renaissance and then back to Roman—as opposed to Greek—antiquity really wanted to say, is—to put it anachronistically for a moment—that freedom should not be understood as a predicate of actions *at all*. Freedom is instead the name of a **status**. *That's* what they wanted us to understand. Their emphasis was not on whether I'm free to do this or that—of course that was important to them—but what was **fundamental** to them was the question, *Do you have the* **status** *of being a free person?* That's the question they're asking.

Once I saw that, I was taken back to the most formative text of all for this way of thinking about freedom, which is the Roman Law. The Roman Law begins by wanting to set up a distinction between two sorts of persons. Because it is a law code, it is asking who is subject to law. It's also a slave society, so not everyone is subject to law—only citizens are subject to law.

Since a citizen is free ex hypothesi, by contrast with being a slave, the question for them is, *What makes a slave a slave?* If you understand what makes a slave, you will understand what it is to be a free person, because to be a free person is *not* to be a slave.

The answer given in the Roman Law to what it is to be a *liber homo*, as they say—using a word we don't have in the English language, 'homo', meaning man or woman—is, just as you would expect, *not* to be dependent upon the arbitrary will of anyone else. Because what it is to be a slave is to be wholly dependent upon the arbitrary will of somebody else.

That's a very deep thought about freedom, because it gets around a paradox which liberal political philosophy often gets into, which is, *If freedom is simply absence of interference, what makes the slave un-free?* There could be a slave who, because the master is benign or absent, is not interfered with in what he or she chooses to do. So what makes him a slave?

But it's not really a puzzle. It's only a puzzle if—

HB: If you look at it in that context.

QS: Exactly. You've *made it into* a puzzle by giving what this tradition would think is a very shallow analysis of the concept of freedom, making it *exclusively* a predicate of actions, whereas what you should think is that it's fundamentally about a human status, the status of not being a dependent.

Questions for Discussion:

1. How do you think "freedom" is generally interpreted in contemporary society?

2. Do you agree with Quentin's implication that a philosopher would naturally be more attracted to the sort of structural symmetry of notions of "presence" and "absence" that appealed to Philip Pettit than intellectual historians? If so, is this a sign of the general disposition of those who opt to pursue philosophy or a consequence of a philosophical training?

3. How does Quentin's forthright recollections of Hannah Arendt's ideas illustrate how modern philosophers influence our understanding of both the past and present? Those interested in a further example of the impact of Hannah Arendt on contemporary political understanding is referred to Chapters 1 and 5 of the Ideas Roadshow conversation **Pants on Fire: On Lying in Politics** *with UC Berkeley intellectual historian Martin Jay.*

II. Presupposing the State
The triumph of the modern liberal view

HB: That brings up what I interpret to be, from reading your works, a key point: to embed this sense of freedom within a larger society. That is to say, if you just look at freedom as being liberated from, or reduced from, any external constraints—this almost naturalistic way of looking at freedom, this idea that you're not holding me or binding me so I can go off in whatever particular direction I choose—one can imagine freedom being defined independently of whatever the state happens to be: there are laws, and these laws are created somehow in some abstract context, and then one is either free or not free depending on that evaluation of that specific criterion.

But if you look instead at what it means to be a free person in accordance with a certain status, then you can begin to make some sort of sensible distinction as to what a free state is, or is not.

QS: This is absolutely fundamental. I could put your point the other way around and say that once I'd come to this realization, it seemed to me that there was something very strange, indeed, even fantastical, about the way that contemporary liberal political philosophy had set up the question of freedom and the state.

Take the kind of liberal political theory that moves in a very strongly libertarian direction as it tends to do in contemporary American political theory, such as Robert Nozick's classic 1974 book, *Anarchy, State, and Utopia*. One begins with the individual who is a possessor of rights; and this person's freedom, in turn, is a right and a means to other rights. Freedom is understood in that text as the absence of coercion.

Let's now think about the state. How does a state characteristically act? It doesn't usually limit our freedom by, as you say, physically taking hold of us. Sure, that might be the case if you're in a court of law and you're handcuffed—someone has taken away your freedom of movement. But that, of course, is not the paradigm of how states operate. The paradigm is that states have laws, there are penalties attached to the breach of those laws, and the aspiration of the legislature is to make you frightened of the consequences of disobedience. That "bends the will," as Jeremy Bentham liked to put it, and a bending of the will is obviously a limiting of choice. And there is your freedom being taken away.

In this liberal model, the state is the immediate and automatic enemy of freedom, because freedom is absence of coercion, but the state is a coercive apparatus. So there's a continual disposition—which Nozick illustrates very well through his book—for this kind of liberal political theory to become anarchistic, because now when you consider the state, you're likely to think to yourself, *Well, is that a legal institution at all? After all, freedom is a fundamental value for me. It's a right and a means to rights—*

HB: *And they're taking it away.*

QS: *And they're taking it away.*
But that is a *fantasy* of the way that we should set up thinking about freedom, because, actually, most of what we talk about when we talk about rights, **presupposes** the state. And the power of this completely different, alternative way of thinking about freedom and what's fundamental about it is that we are **in** the state.

HB: Otherwise, we're in a "state of nature", as it were—

QS: Well, yes. We're in a fantasy state of nature. It's not a sociological condition. It's just a thought experiment.
Now, I do want to say something that is likely to be misunderstood. You picked this up beautifully in your comments earlier.

I am not saying that if you now handcuff me, you *haven't* taken away an element of my freedom. Of course not. If we were to get up from our conversation and find that the door was locked, then we would not be free to leave the room. We would have the power, but somebody unknown to us would have taken that power away—of course we would then be unfree to leave: we had that power counterfactually, but it has been taken away from us.

What the writers I'm interested in want to say is, *"Well, we're not denying that. What we're denying is that **that's** what's fundamental about freedom. That's making it a predicate of actions. But it's the name of a **status**. Fundamentally, it's **not** a predicate of actions. It's the name of a status."*

HB: One of the things that captivated me as I was reading your writings was how these ideas were eventually replaced by our classical liberal understanding.

It's as if there was a war going on between two fundamental ideas of freedom: one, according to which freedom is associated with a fundamental status—this neo-Roman view—and another, a more naturalistic, inhibitory sense of freedom as a natural predicate to action.

And there are times when this first view, this neo-Roman or republican view was to the fore. During the English Civil Wars, for example, you point out that there were those who were advocating precisely this idea of freedom as a way of justifying the elimination of the monarchy.

But eventually, somehow, this neo-Roman view of freedom was supplanted by the classical liberal view that simply regards freedom as a predicate to action. In fact, the triumph of this classical liberal view was so thorough, that—I believe you quote Isaiah Berlin at some point here—it was as if it was impossible to even contemplate any other view of freedom. Is that a fair depiction, or am I missing something?

QS: I think that's a very fair outline. Let me respond a little bit to exactly that point. The history, as I see it, is one of very strong contestation in the early modern period. The gradual disappearance of the neo-Roman view as a candidate for thinking about freedom, and its replacement by the—as we now know it—liberal understanding of freedom as simply non-interference with actions—yes, there is a historical story to be told about that; and that is roughly how I see it.

Questions for Discussion:

1. In what ways can the notion of inalienable human rights be re-expressed in the language of freedom as a form of status?

2. What do you think the neo-Roman view of freedom implied for how society viewed suicide in those societies?

3. To what extent does the act of presupposing the prior existence of a specific type of state possibly explain the evolution of our understanding of freedom from the neo-Roman to the modern liberal view?

III. The Perils of Arbitrary Power
Becoming a slave

HB: I'm not a political philosopher and clearly don't claim otherwise. But as I was reading this, I was thinking, *Quentin Skinner tells me that this view is by and large the triumphant view and that this sense of freedom as a predicate to action—"freedom" as meaning unencumbered to act rather than linked to a sense of status—is the way that people now generally understand the term.* But hang on a minute. When I watch the news, when I turn on CNN, I notice that very often people talk in such a way as to equate political freedom with democracy. In other words, they seem to explicitly link freedom with the notion of how a state is being governed.

Perhaps I should back up a bit to see if I can state my point as clearly as possible. The classic liberal understanding, as I understand it, is that government makes the laws, and it doesn't really make any difference how the laws are being made in terms of our definition of freedom: these are the laws that define our freedom in terms of whether or not we conform to those laws, or whether we don't—or, as Hobbes would say, whether we form a covenant with those particular laws—in other words, whether we buy into those laws.

So insofar as we allow these laws to constrain us, we are limiting our freedom vis-à-vis these particular laws and we all live in a society with laws that constrain our actions. It's not a matter of whether we are considered free by disposition or status or free in the sense of belonging to a "free state" or anything like that—it's just that our sense of being free, or not free, is defined with respect to these laws, with respect to how we are permitted to act. And that claim, as I understand it, has been so successful in terms of its acceptance that people even question how you can look at freedom in any other way.

But then I turn on CNN and people are saying things like, "*We have to make the world safe for democracy,*" and, "*This is the only way to protect your freedom.*"

So it seems to me that the general public, at least, **does** actually look at things somewhat differently, insofar as we **do** make an equivalence between a sense of freedom and a particular form of government.

So maybe, at least in the worlds that I travel in, this idea of freedom as a predicate to action independent of whatever form of government one adopts to make the laws is not quite as universally accepted as one might suppose.

QS: Yes. That's very interesting. You're absolutely right to stress the distinction between, let me call it "the liberal view"—which is a slight parody—in contrast with the neo-Roman view. The former view is not very interested in the relation of liberty to forms of government, and the latter thinks that there is one canonical form of government, namely democracy, which alone delivers freedom.

Now, what **I'm** struck by, with regard to talk about the relation of freedom to democracy in the United States, is that the freedom that is prized is the freedom to be left alone to do what you want. And democracy is prized as a form of government that will enable that to happen: "*He governs best who governs least.*" It's a democratic framework, but the aspiration that people have within that framework is to maximize their freedom of action.

When I started my research all those years ago, I was reading people who were saying, "*Unless you are yourself active in the political sphere, this will be dangerous to your own liberty.*" These are the **real** democrats, because what they're saying is that there's a canonical form of government—which is self-government—and the reason that that *alone* secures your freedom is that what your freedom **is**, is *not* being subject to arbitrary power as a member of a civil association.

How can you minimize arbitrary power? Well, only by making, in some way, the law be a reflection of your will, or at least of your represented will. If you can see in the law either your will or a representation of it, then in obeying the law you are obeying your will. Thus there is a sense in which you are free in obeying the law: namely, it's the law that you think it should be.

HB: It's *your* law, as it were.

QS: Exactly. The term "autonomous" says it all: it comes from the Greek for "giving the law to yourself". That's what it is to be autonomous.

Well, within what political framework can you give the law to yourself? **Only** a framework in which you are *actively* able to participate, or to participate by representation, in a deliberative and representative series of assemblies which are the sole source of law. That *alone* does it. That is why in the Roman Republican, and then in the Renaissance Republican, understandings of the state, it is *this* view of freedom which is being claimed—and it requires a particular state.

Which exact state, then, does it require? These writers are very clear that it has to have two conditions attached to it.

First, *only* law must rule. There must be no discretionary powers. There must be no executive powers that can simply be invoked. There must be no royal prerogative such that the will of the monarch suddenly becomes the law. All discretionary powers are arbitrary because they're somebody's will. But they have to be my will, or my represented will, so they are all excluded—they enslave.

And secondly, as I've already said, I must be able to see my will in the law.

What this mandates is a particular form of a very active democratic citizenship as a *condition* of upholding freedom, but not as a condition of upholding freedom as being left alone to do whatever I want.

The freedom that is being upheld is freedom from arbitrary power, because if you're not free from arbitrary power, you don't have freedom in this absolutely fundamental sense.

HB: And just to add to that, as you point out explicitly in your writings, in order to damage this sense of freedom, this arbitrary power doesn't actually have to be used; it just has to exist with the *potential* that it could be used. Because even if it exists *potentially*, then it will, to some degree at least, rot the society from within: then you get these sycophants and courtiers and so forth.

If the laws can be perverted according to arbitrary will, then an entire societal superstructure arises which threatens the fundamental freedom—by this definition—of individuals.

QS: This is absolutely right; and I think this is really fundamental. Another way of putting this, which brings out the contrast that I'm interested in between the liberal understanding of freedom and this other way of thinking about it, is to insist that freedom is not de facto.

Earlier in our conversation we were saying that the liberal view is that freedom is a de facto idea. The question is, *Is somebody now stopping you from doing something?* If not—if it's within your power to do that thing—then you're free to do it.

What the other theory is trying to get you to see is the *hidden* operations of power to constrain us. They are *not* de facto. These hidden operations of power don't actually have to operate for us to be less free.

And I think to make that clear, I ought to say a little bit more about how this notion of not being subject to arbitrary power fills out. Because what these writers want to say about the person who *is* subject to the arbitrary will of somebody else is that—well, first of all, that person is a slave. For us, that would just be a metaphor; we're not talking about chattel slavery. But they would speak of this as living like a slave in certain domains of your life.

Now, how do they make that rather melodramatic claim come good? The answer is in two ways.

The first is a kind of metaphysical point, but it's one that's very important. If you are dependent on somebody else's will, it doesn't even have to be the case that you're aware of that. This is a point you've just made. That's absolutely fundamental. You could be a slave without knowing it.

So, for example, in a slave society, you could be born a slave. You may not know that you're a slave, but you are. Now, it's perfectly true that you couldn't be a slave for long in any domain of your life without coming to see that, but the first point that these writers want to make is that, in that existential condition, no action of yours is ever freely performed, because an action freely performed is an action performed according to your will. And a free choice is the choice that you will.

Of course this may all be determined somehow—we're not talking here about determinism—but it's a compatibilist view that the experience of having these capacities to chose is existential.

So that's **one** criterion for being able to choose and act freely. And it's not merely necessary; it's sufficient.

Now, if you are subject to arbitrary power, there's always going to be a second criterion for you being able to act: that the person with arbitrary power to stop you has chosen not to exercise that arbitrary power. It's *always* there. They could always exercise it.

HB: And it's their choice.

QS: And it's their choice. They can exercise that choice with impunity, and there's nothing you can do about it. So, when you act you have this illusion of freedom, which is actually based upon the non-exercise of hidden power.

And what I want to alert us to in our own society is the extent to which there are these hidden powers.

That sounds paranoid. But there are these arbitrary powers, which means that much of what we do is only done with permission.

HB: I don't think that sounds paranoid, and here's why. If you look at this in a modern context, and you look closely at what we call democracies in this day and age and examine how the laws are actually made and who is really in charge, the question is, *Is there something analogous to sycophancy of the courtiers to the king in our present-day democracy?* It could be political action committees or hugely wealthy individuals who donate influential amounts to political parties, or what have you. And by this definition, you could make a judgement as to the amount of freedom that exists in this context, even in a so-called democratic society.

QS: Very much so.

HB: And then you could look right now at a country like China, for example. Again, you can go deeper and further than just saying, *"There are laws. Are the laws actually being applied? What are the individual liberties vis-à-vis these external constraints that citizens have?"* and instead start asking probing questions about **how** those laws get made. How does environmental legislation in China happen right now, for example? Is that an arbitrary process?

QS: Or maybe *all* their laws are arbitrary.

HB: Exactly. So it seems to me that these questions are very topical and quite pertinent to a number of questions about civil liberties that are deeply relevant to what is happening in the contemporary world.

QS: I hope so. These are very apropos remarks, and they enable me to move on from the first to the second of the points I want to make about spelling out this notion of freedom as an absence of arbitrary power.

The first point I was talking about was that you actually *never* act autonomously if there is identifiable arbitrary power.

But the second point is the one that you've now just made: it's not likely that if you are dependent upon someone in any domain of your life that you will live for long without coming to recognize that, and the implications of that.

Suppose, since we're sitting right now in the middle of an American university, that you're a junior professor without tenure. It's very hard to imagine that that doesn't, in some way, affect your character, a whole range of your actions towards your superiors, towards your peers, and so on.

This is all summarized in a rather brutal epigram by the Roman writers, by saying, *"Slaves are slavish."* How can you *not* be slavish if you're a slave? It's a character-forming horror. So the idea that if you live in servitude you will find that you're a servile character, is one that they're very keen on. It's almost *impossible* for that not to be the case.

So here's the thought: in relation to these hidden exercises of power—and this is the horror of slavery, even living like a slave in just some domain of your life—**you don't know what might happen**.

And that's going to be true if the laws are made arbitrarily. I would guess that this must be something that happens a lot in China. The laws are not made in a democratic fashion—they are the will of a party that is imposing them on the country—so you don't always know, I imagine, what might happen to you if you were to speak out. Maybe nothing, but *you don't know*. But if you don't know, you won't speak out—or you'd be a very, very brave person if you do.

That must be the position—somewhat modified and less serious perhaps—of the assistant professor without tenure. *Do I speak out if the chair of the department has just summoned a meeting and has talked nonsense? Do I **say** that this is nonsense?* Well, you'll think carefully about it.

HB: There's something else that might well be mentioned here about such a structure. Again, let's take the assistant professor aiming for tenure. Once the professor *does* manage to get tenure, there's often a tendency to ensure that the entire system doesn't change so that this state of servility is imposed on future generations. There seems to be a self-perpetuating nature to all of this sort of thing: *"I went through this so you have to go through this too."*

QS: Well, that would be a great professional deformation.

But I think the general structure of what we're talking about is an affront to **freedom**. It's an affront to freedom in this silent way, because what is the mechanism that we're talking about here? It is self-censorship. But self-censorship is, of course, censorship. It's a form of censorship.

This is what I mean by saying that the operations of power which worry me are the silent ones that stem from the fact that those with arbitrary power over us don't even have to make it clear to us that they have this power and could exercise it. *We* know that; and *they* know that *we* know. It affects how people conduct themselves all the time. It systemically corrodes freedom.

Questions for Discussion:

1. Can you point to instances in your past when your behaviour has been compromised as a result of fear of some arbitrary power as Quentin describes?

2. Do some aspects of contemporary society, such as the military or a corporate environment, mandate that its subjects "act slavishly"?

3. Do you agree with Howard that many Americans regard the adoption of "American-style" democracy as a form of status?

4. To what extent is it possible to have a clearly enunciated framework of laws that you can be assured will always be applied in a consistently regular fashion and yet they are not "your own"? How would such a scenario fit into Quentin's categorization procedure?

IV. Freedom, Applied
Contemporary politics through the lens of arbitrary power

HB: I know this is not your job, but I'm going to ask you to speculate a little bit. I'd like to continue to focus on some practical implications of your ideas.

Let's pretend I'm the President of the United States and I say to you, "*Quentin, congratulations, I'm making you my Secretary of State because you're somebody who deeply understands this pivotal idea of freedom. Help me make my way forward in the contemporary world.*" What would you do, or what might you do differently?

QS: Well, I am struck by the monarchical structures of American political society, as I see it now. The President is up against a terrible problem, which is a feature of the American Constitution, which is that it's hard to get anything systematic done. That can be presented as a glory of the American Constitution by contrast with the first-past-the-post system, such as we have in the United Kingdom. There, by contrast, you can relatively easily get a social revolution put through, as was done by Mrs. Thatcher, where the largest majority that ever voted for her was 37% of the people. That can't happen in the United States. We can get more things done, but not all the things that we get done are things that we should have wanted to get done.

HB: Right. Stalin got things done too.

QS: Yes. So the glory of the American Constitution is to make it difficult to get things done. But there is also a large reservoir of executive power that enables things to happen when the Congress won't enable them to happen. The great exponent of that, the greatest radical

President, was, I suppose, FDR. The number of executive orders by which he ruled, especially in the course of the Second World War, was enormous. It must have run into the thousands.

But there you have a problem for a democracy; and we have it in the United Kingdom in a somewhat different form, in the form of the royal prerogative. The royal prerogative is, of course, in the hands of the executive for the time being, but it places enormous discretionary power in the hands of the Prime Minister.

When Britain was taken into war in Iraq by Tony Blair in 2003, he didn't ask the Parliament and he didn't have to ask the Parliament. He did it, and he subsequently had a vote on it, but *subsequently.*

He was, of right, exercising the royal prerogative of war and peace as the Prime Minister of the country. But the fact remains that doing so was an act of arbitrary power. Both of these two democracies have enormous reserves of arbitrary power in them.

To take the Tony Blair case, because it was a very moving one, a million people walked through the center of London with placards that said, "*Not in our name.*" That's to say, this is not a democratic procedure at all.

HB: These are not our laws.

QS: These are not our laws. Indeed—this isn't a law at all. People have intuitions about this way of thinking about freedom which I want them to bring out and think about much more.

Yes, indeed, it was not in your name, because this had not been passed by your representative will. They had no say in this, and yet this became the policy of the state. And, of course, it was a disastrous policy.

HB: So one concrete measure, then, would be to eliminate the royal prerogative in the UK?

QS: Yes. I don't know why this isn't a big issue in my country. I think that what my eminent colleague, Jeremy Waldron calls "the dignity of legislation" is something that we have to think more about in democracies: what's meant to rule is the represented will of the people. That's one thing that worries me very much.

The state, then—which we absolutely need, and, of course, is the means to the freedom that we've been talking about—is perpetually liable to become the problem instead of the solution. The state is meant to be the solution, but we give it so much power that we can make it into the problem. That's the unavoidable paradox of the fact that we all live in states.

But more than that, I worry about the fragility of states in relation to the arbitrary powers to which they're subjected. Consider the position of a third world country that is trying to attract internal investment. The corporations that wish to invest want to be able to set the terms of investment and employment, and maybe to be given a bit of leeway about environmental legislation.

All of this happens. Why does it happen? Because these countries are totally dependent upon these external players. And that dependence can mean that things that are contrary to the common good of that community have to be done in order to attract the money to keep the community running.

HB: Yet again it's a kind of sycophancy relationship.

QS: Yes, it's a sycophancy relationship. Moreover, we could generalize that, I think, into a view about international relations. It seems to me that an honourable way of thinking about international relations would be to seek to minimize these sycophancy relations. That's to say, to seek to minimize the dependence upon the arbitrary will of extremely rich countries, which must be the day-to-day experience of very poor countries.

HB: So that would lead to a greater sense of parity, a greater sense of national independence within, perhaps, a global decision-making structure?

QS: That would be the hope. It would be a view of freedom. It would be a moral aspiration, a moral aspiration of the rich countries to minimize the extent to which their relationships with poor countries are actually of this arbitrary kind.

I'm trying to see freedom entirely, at its foundation, as a question about how to avoid arbitrary power. If we go back to the model of politics that this would generate, notice that it would be a politics in which each person is, by the state—which would have to help to do this—liberated from the exercise of arbitrary power within their lives.

Some of these forms of arbitrary power have become much worse during my own lifetime. One very important instance is the de-unionization of workforces in the name of something called "'the free market", reflective of some notion of freedom that is clearly not the one that I'm talking to you about this afternoon.

If you completely de-unionize, of course you can get more efficient workforces, but what you're also doing is making those workforces completely dependent upon you.

Now consider the plight of migrant workforces, which may often be comprised of people who are illegally in the country in which they are working. What chance have they of a decent wage? What chance have they of negotiating their wage? None at all. They're completely dependent upon someone who offers them work; and if they don't want it, then there's no negotiation about the terms of it.

HB: And, in fact, they can easily be manipulated. It's like *The Grapes of Wrath*.

QS: Yes, it looks awfully like that terrifying novel. To me it is a shocking fact that, in the name of "freedom", we have increased dependence. On my account, to increase dependence is to diminish freedom.

HB: Is this danger of increased dependency as a threat to freedom something that you feel people are sufficiently aware of? You alluded just now to the curious usage of the word "free" in the context of "the free market". which instead increases dependency and thus leads to an actual *diminishment* of freedom.

For a long time there was this mantra that people were chanting, at least in the developed world, that free markets are the way of the future, and that anybody who believes anything to the contrary is just being wilfully obdurate and doesn't have any common sense—this "end-of-history" view that this is necessarily where the world is going so you better accept it and prosper or fall by the wayside.

Is it your view that the economic crisis of 2008 and its prolonged aftermath might lead people to reconsider previous dogmas and instead move in different sorts of directions? Or not?

QS: Very interesting. I don't know if it's to be attributed to the crisis of 2008 and its aftermath, but the idea that what I've been talking about captures something absolutely fundamental about the experience of freedom of choice and being a free person, is, I think, more prevalent. The more I talk to people about it, the more I hear people respond, "*Yes, I see what you're saying.*"

One way in which this has come up recently is the discovery that we all made within the last year, that both in the United Kingdom and in the United States, it's probable that agents of the state are reading all our emails.

Now, this has been constructed in both these countries as a problem about privacy. And it's true that President Obama, honourably enough, has noted that it's an obvious affront to privacy. Nobody denies that. It's an affront to privacy if you read my emails without my permission.

HB: Tautologically.

QS: That's right. But the payoff is supposed to be security. Now, I'm saying that's the wrong way to phrase it. This is an affront to *freedom*, because once I'm aware that agents of the state may be reading all my emails, I may start to write very different sorts of emails. I may stop writing emails altogether.

HB: You may even start thinking differently.

QS: I *will* start thinking differently. I'll start thinking, *What will happen if they read this? Maybe I should rephrase this. Maybe I should leave that bit out.*

These are not questions about privacy; these are questions about freedom of speech. I'm having my freedom of speech taken away in a silent, insidious way that doesn't make it *seem* as if my freedom of speech is being taken away, because nobody is stopping me, no one is interfering directly with me writing the emails I want to write. But again, that's the way of thinking about freedom superficially. That's surface stuff.

What we're talking about is something much more fundamental, which is, a democratic citizen thinking, *Well, I don't know if I can really say this anymore.* And that's the point: ***I don't know***. That's what it is to live like a slave in a certain domain, which is, you *don't know* what might happen to you.

HB: That's a very concrete example. Exactly as you said, it's not as if you're being *physically* impeded or coerced, but at the same time the knowledge of this arbitrary nature *does* limit your freedom.

QS: I'm sure it does. I don't do anything very sensitive, and I'm not an important person, but if either of those were different, I'm sure I would not be using email in a great range of areas—not because I know something terrible will happen to me, but because I *don't* know what *might* happen to me. But that is a clear instance of freedom being taken away. And that's what I really want to stress: these silent operations of power in our democracies.

To go back to what you were saying about the economic crisis, I must first say that what has happened, I think, simply explodes libertarianism. Because, after all, who saved us from begging in the streets? The states saved us. Individual states came forward.

I was living in the United States at the time, and I remember watching President Bush. He didn't dare say, "*The state is doing this.*" But he said, "*We've got to save our commonwealth. We've got to save our republic.*" What was happening was that states came forward as lenders of last resort. And without our permission, or indeed the permission of our grandchildren who are still going to be paying off this debt, they said, "*We'll face it. We'll simply take on that debt.*" In fact, nobody else could say that. So what is all this hostility to the state in this kind of libertarianism? We're all living in states, and what we want to do is to make them properly democratic states.

One of the powers of the theory that we're talking about this afternoon is that it connects freedom extremely strongly to equality. It says that what it is to be a free citizen is to be *equally* free with all other citizens, to be able to have this sense of belonging such that I feel that the law is a representation of my will.

It isn't, of course, literally *my* will, and I may be in the minority, but if I'm in the minority and I feel that the structure is right, I think, *Well, you can't win everything*.

But I've got to be able to see my represented will in the law, and so have you. We are equal citizens. We have equal rights in respect of the direction of the polity. That is to say that we are instantiating freedom as non-dependence.

But it is also to say that a political society that instantiates that value has instantiated social justice. Because what is social justice except the equal freedom of citizens in that way?

HB: Let me be devil's advocate and pick up on this point of social justice. Allow me to take an extreme, ridiculous example to demonstrate a point. Let's imagine a state that is fully democratic, where the will of the people is such that everyone can feel that they are responsible for crafting the laws. And imagine that one of the laws that is arrived at through this democratic and open process is that all intellectual historians shall be sent off to the Gulags.

This does not strike me as a law which incorporates any genuine sense of social justice, not simply because I happen to like intellectual historians—which I most certainly do—but because I am appealing to a higher sense of justice that goes beyond this so-called tyranny of the majority.

But in your view, or at least in my understanding of this view of what it means to be free in a state where everyone has an equal role to play, such laws can, in principle, be passed. It is not the arbitrary will of one monarch who has decreed this. Can we really define social justice this way?

QS: This raises a very big question for anyone who's started to take this way of thinking about freedom, and therefore equal citizenship, seriously. What institutions would we need to design to deliver this kind of equal freedom? The problem that democracy constantly faces is majoritarianism.

I spoke earlier about the Thatcherite social experiment, which permanently changed a number of crucial institutions of my society. I never voted for that. I didn't approve of it. I still think that a lot of it was disastrous. My opinion was not asked.

Of course, then, majoritarianism can be an enemy of freedom in the way that we're talking about. And your fantasy example would, as it happens, be particularly disturbing for me personally.

So the short answer to your doubt is naturally the problem that we all face as democrats, which is that, prima facie, democracy is simply majoritarian creed; and we mustn't let it be so.

What, then, are we saying? We are saying that the ideal constitution that will deliver freedom in the form I'm talking about, and thus social justice would have to have institutions that were not elective institutions. It would have to have agreed but non-elective supervising legal institutions that could do something to mitigate those dangers.

HB: And represent minority rights in this case, or the rights of individuals.

QS: That's the great issue: how do we represent minority rights under a majoritarian system? In the United States, the Constitution is actually rather sensitive to that; less so in my country. But if we were now designing the ideal constitution, that's one of the first things we would have to think about.

I'm not a constitutional lawyer, but one of the things that I've come to feel strongly about in my recent thinking about this way of talking about freedom and social justice is that we probably need a very different constitution. We probably need to think again about central features of our constitution and what kind of a freedom we are trying to instantiate. And, by the way, it might be quite prudent to start thinking about this now.

In the name of a freedom that is understood as the freedom of markets to do whatever they need to produce rising living standards, the position has now been reached in the United States where a very substantial proportion of the entire wealth of the country is earned by 1% of the population. This is an extraordinary level of social inequality, and it's similar in my country.

HB: And it's growing worse.

QS: In both countries it's very grave; and in both countries it's growing worse. There are several things we might want to ask about that. One very interesting point, which has been thrown up by a great deal of research in Scandinavian countries that have much greater social equality, much higher levels of direct taxation, is that these countries regularly register a higher approval of their society by the citizens of that society than do the United Kingdom or the United States. The latest statistics issued by the United Nations tell us that Denmark is the happiest country in the world. Well, it has a direct taxation rate in the 50s. That's quite interesting.

But more interesting, perhaps, because it's not anecdotal, is all the economic research that's been done on the Nordic countries about the connection between economic equality and efficiency. Which is to say that it may be that these high and rising rates of economic inequality, and the instinct to prefer the preservation of economic rights over other different kinds of rights—which is true in the European Union, just as it's true in the United States—may not be the way to go for efficiency. It's also worth just asking ourselves whether, if it continues at this rate, the social fabric may not begin to tear.

HB: You allude, quite neatly I think, to another point that you made earlier: that a full sense of freedom, in the way you're describing it, might actually be in the comprehensive long term interests of the state.

One can imagine that there's a large-scale individual psychological price to be paid throughout a society where this doesn't exist: people may be less secure, less creative, less productive. But this, in turn, makes one wonder about how the overall interests of the state are served by a society where an arbitrary will is present.

Earlier, you mentioned Machiavelli and others who were constantly talking about how to best proceed in order to have the greatest possible state.

Now, "the greatest possible state" in Renaissance Florence might well mean one that is conquering and subjugating other city states. But when you began talking about Scandinavia, I started to think that it could well be that, because you have a much greater level of personal empowerment throughout that society, because you have much less of this diminution of personal freedom and consequently greater equality, the interests of the body politic are served not only in terms of their own sense of freedom and entitlement, but also economically.

That is, aside altogether from whatever moral arguments we might choose to make, it could well be that it is in the best economic interest of the state of Denmark to have the sort of society they have, whereas it is *not* in the best interest of the United States of America or the United Kingdom to have the sort of wealth inequality that they have. It is only in the best interest of that tiny minority of people who have the resources to perpetuate that.

QS: I agree with you. Well, what we have to face is that the United Kingdom and the United States have become very oligarchic. It's just not possible to imagine that the kind of inequalities—which are not merely tolerated but are growing in both countries—would not run into tremendous political pressure in the Scandinavian social democracies, where notions of equality of citizenship are very strongly entrenched and where the rights that are entrenched are not primarily economic rights, but are instead rights of citizenship. Then it's a very interesting question about whether that may be more economically efficient, but there's no doubt that it's more just.

And that is apparently what people feel. It's quite fascinating. If you look at this happiness measure, which has been done in a quite sophisticated way in recent years, neither the United Kingdom nor the United States are in the top 10. But all the Scandinavian countries are in the top 10. So this makes you think.

Questions for Discussion:

1. In what ways can our modern democracies be improved to increase the confidence of citizens that the laws of the land are "theirs"? Might there be some concrete measures that can be devised through modern technology to ensure that citizens interact more regularly with policymakers and legislators than simply voting every few years?

2. Does it logically follow from Quentin's argument that an increasing socio-economic gap between rich and poor is an affront to freedom?

3. To what extent does the standard American conservative rhetoric about "economic opportunity" regard "freedom" as solely a predicate to (economic) action, with "government regulation" representing a potential constraint on such action that should be avoided?

4. Do you agree that government surveillance represents a threat to your freedom?

5. How might Quentin's concern of the dependency of poorer countries on richer countries be addressed within the sphere of international relations? How, concretely, could NGOs and intergovernmental bodies act together to concretely minimize this potential dependency?

6. In what ways might "happiness measures" be reinterpreted as "the extent to which citizens feel independent from arbitrary powers"?

V. Rhetoric

Closely examining another classical Roman idea

HB: I'd like to switch gears a little bit and talk about rhetoric and persuasion, which is another research interest of yours. How does that fit in, if at all, with these notions of liberty that we've been talking about? Is there a link somehow, or is it something completely separate?

QS: Well, there *is* a link, but it's a quite elaborate one. I first got interested in the classical theory of rhetoric and its uses in later cultures through looking at the politics of Renaissance city-states, which were highly democratic politics. Of course, they were patriarchal politics—we're only talking about a grand council of heads of families. But if you go to any of the city republics of Tuscany, even nowadays, you see these gigantic halls—particularly in Venice—which contained the electorate of the city. And when they met in council, this was the group that determined war and peace and levels of taxation, and so forth.

How did they actually operate? Well, speeches were made, and sometimes these speeches lasted several days. The council would be in session for several days while questions of war and peace, in particular, could be determined by the *popolo*. But the quality that was absolutely at a premium was eloquent public speaking. You had to have a loud voice, know how to move people's emotions and how to optimally marshal an effective argument.

All of these issues are addressed in the Roman rhetorical tradition. The Roman rhetorical tradition was more about judicial rhetoric than deliberative rhetoric: it was not so much a rhetoric for deliberative assemblies. But in its revival in the Renaissance, the question of how to persuade a multitude came to be absolutely fundamental.

There are two arenas in which you're trying to persuade your fellow citizens: deliberative assemblies and a court of law in front of the "twelve good men and true" who are trying a case. They are the ultimate arbiters. You've got to persuade them to see things your way.

I thus became very interested in the genre of textbooks in antiquity which purported to show you how to move a jury, or a judge, or a set of judges; or how to move a representative assembly.

Now, you could say this is a thoroughly sinister skill because, as Aristotle would put it, this is where *logos* stops, where reasoning stops, and *pathos* takes over: the arousing of the emotions.

But what the authors of these books want to say is, "*Yes, but what we're doing is arousing the emotions for the* **right** *course or the* **correct** *verdict.*" So there's a constant tension there. I became very interested in the role of that notion of persuasion in Renaissance culture.

I've written two books about this now (*Reason and Rhetoric in the Philosophy of Hobbes* and *Forensic Shakespeare*). I first became interested in this in relation to the all-out attack on rhetorical argument that was launched during the scientific revolution.

You could say that the scientific revolution of the 17th century was, in part, an attack on this kind of rhetorical culture, because what it sought to do was to tie truth not to persuasion, but to *certainty*—to make truth, as it were, algorithmic: there would be certain principles that were laid down that were principles of reasoning, and if these were correctly followed then you'll arrive at the truths which could not be debated by the other side.

HB: Although ironically, perhaps, Galileo himself used these wonderful rhetorical devices in his *Dialogues*.

QS: Indeed. He, of course, is a Renaissance philosopher and he's passionately interested in the fact that—as the rhetoricians always say and we still think in a court of law—"there are two sides to the question".

There's the case of the prosecution, but there's also a case for the defense, and both may have a lot of logos on their side. We've got to hear this out, and then we've got to see how to weigh that.

But that's not what Descartes is interested in doing, that's not what Hobbes is interested in doing, nor what Leibniz is interested in doing. These people are all mathematicians, and they want to privilege mathematics as the model of knowledge. What *they* want are axioms that lead to certainty.

So there's a *total* repudiation of the idea that knowledge might not have that form—that it might be that there's *always* the possibility of arguing the other side and that the relationship of persuasion to truth is there in the rhetorical tradition because it's there in our theory of knowledge. But what they did was to reject that model of knowledge in favour of this, as I'm calling it, "algorithmic" idea that knowledge should be tied to certainty.

HB: And if you look at Spinoza, if you look at *The Ethics*, say, it seems to me that he's *deliberately* invoking a mathematical structure for exactly this reason. It's almost like a slap in the face to any attempt at rhetorical devices.

QS: That's precisely what it is. Historically, it is a slap in the face. He says *more geometrico*—that ethics *has* to be done in the manner of geometry, which sounds ludicrous to a Renaissance philosopher.

So I wrote a book about the collapse of rhetoric in the face of this. I've centered it on the figure of Hobbes, who is a mighty rhetorician, but who is using it *against* rhetorical culture.

But now I've written a second book, which is about dramaturgy, because it seems to me that in Renaissance culture the greatest arena for rhetoric and the presentation of many voices around some issue is the drama.

In the English language, the teaching of rhetoric in schools and universities was the Renaissance revival of classical antiquity—if there's one thing that is directly revived, it is Roman rhetoric. Then you might ask yourself, "*Well, is it an accident that only a generation later you had the greatest efflorescence of English writings of a dramatic kind?"*

There's never been anything like it. In one generation, you have Ben Jonson and Shakespeare, Webster, Tourneur, and Marlowe, and on and on it goes. You cannot replicate that in any period of English-language writing. But it is exactly the period in which rhetoric was seen to be the fundamental human science.

This is how I got interested in the relation of rhetoric to dramaturgy. I chose Shakespeare—why not go for the top?—and what I find is that in a number of his plays, and at a certain point in his intellectual development, the plays that he wants to write are judicial, in the sense that they draw systematically on the principles of argument laid down in the rhetorical handbooks of antiquity.

It's now impossible for me *not* to believe that either he had an extraordinary memory for his schooling—which would have been centered on these rhetorical handbooks that he would have known by heart—or that he had one of them open on the desk as he was writing.

Take two predicaments you could be in. Perhaps there's something that you want me to believe and it's false. Rhetoricians aren't interested in truth, but in *seeming* to be true: verisimilitude. How can you make something that is false seem true? Well, the rhetoricians will tell you that they have a number of very precise rules about how to make the false seem true.

Now think of Shakespeare and that great drama where there's a character whose whole purpose is to make the false seem true: the figure of Iago in Othello. He wants Othello to believe that his wife is having an adulterous affair. It's false, but he makes Othello believe that it's true. How does he do it?

He does it according to all the rules that are laid out in these classical handbooks. If you read the classical handbook and then you read Iago, you find that you're reading the classical handbook again, but turned into this extraordinary verse.

Here's a second dilemma you might be in. There's something that you want me to believe is true. And it *is* true. But at the moment *nobody* believes it's true.

And again the rhetoricians say, "*Oh yes, that's quite common.*" The question is how to make the truth *seem* true. It *is* true, but no one believes it, so you've got to make it seem true. The fact that it is true is not actually what's important. How do you make the truth seem true?

Now consider the dilemma of the ghost in Hamlet. He's just been murdered, but nobody believes that he's been murdered. Everyone believes that he was stung by a serpent. He's got to make Hamlet, his son, believe the truth, which no one currently believes. How does he do that? Once more, if you read the ghost's great speeches to Hamlet, you'll find that you're reading these great rhetorical textbooks.

HB: But this very notion of making the truth seem true would presumably be anathema to these rationalist philosophers we were talking about earlier.

QS: They hate it. Because for them the truth is conspicuous: "Two and two is four" is the paradigm case of a truth.

HB: And if you can't see it—

QS: Well, then they think, *Okay, well, let's just tell you about numbers and then you'll see this is a paradigm of truth.*

Now, you could think that our culture went in a wrong direction here, because very often it's important that we should be able to make the truth seem true. How do we make it seem to be true, especially if people don't believe it to be true? That seems to be an important question to ask.

HB: And looking at contemporary society, do you think that there has been a precipitous drop in our collective rhetorical abilities?

QS: That's such an interesting question. Well, we're brought up to think "yes", because we think of the extraordinary oratorical powers that were brought to bear in the writing of the American Constitution, in the debating of that Constitution. We think of how those powers were valued and how important it was to present issues in the right way.

And, of course, these were persuasive efforts. You could read them in print, because both the Anti-Federalist Papers and the Federalist Papers are telling us two views about the Constitution. It's very interesting to read the anti-federalists. They have extremely strong arguments to offer about states' rights and the danger of arbitrary power if the republic is too large. Madison has got to reply to these, but both of these are densely rhetorical texts.

And in England, we're used to the idea that when matters of state were decided on the floor of the House of Commons, these skills were of paramount importance. Now they're very rarely decided there, just as in this country. Things aren't really decided on the floor of Congress.

I think we feel that these skills in deliberative assemblies have atrophied. Whether they've atrophied in the courts, I don't know, but it would be interesting to know if courts trained young lawyers in these forensic skills in the way that they were trained classically and in the Renaissance, in the books that purport to tell you how to do it.

HB: But it seems to me that there's another aspect that might get lost alongside a decline in these specific rhetorical skills. Let's suppose that there has been some degree of widespread atrophying of these skills. You were speaking before of this ability to create arguments, to look at things from both sides, and I submit to you that there might be an aspect of tolerance that is associated with that.

If one loses the skills necessary to be able to present a position from both sides, then that might enhance the likelihood that one might start looking at positions in a polarized way.

Which is to say that there might be an argument that rhetorical skills are linked to a broader intellectual development that is associated with a certain sense of tolerance. Is that a fair assessment, do you think?

QS: I like that very much. Well, let me be frank with you; I think that anglophone culture went off the rails in the 17th century in this particular respect. The idea that we should tie knowledge to certainty, and that what we should be trying to do is to make sure that we can move from premises to conclusions in a form that leaves no opening for debate—that image of public debate, and indeed that self-image of philosophy, seems to me to be profoundly destructive.

If you think of an earlier phase in the writing of especially moral and political philosophy, it was very common for such works to be written in the form of dialogues. And why is that? Well, because there are two sides to the question. I think of David Hume's *Dialogues Concerning Natural Religion*, in which four or five figures come together to debate the existence of God. And it's quite well understood that there are different points of view. One person leaves because he can't tolerate this, but the others *are* tolerant. And the reason they're tolerant is that they recognize that the truth is not all going to be in one direction.

That rings true to me from my professional and personal experience. As a senior academic who has sat on many committees at a number of different universities, I can say that it's extremely rare for the set-up to be one in which it's completely clear what the outcome is going to be ahead of time.

We're all deliberating. Many of us have different points of view. We come to think, in the course of the meeting, *Well, I may vote in a different way here; I hadn't really appreciated that side of it*. It may not be that I didn't know something, but rather that I didn't weigh it correctly.

I don't want to romanticize this. I'm actually just making a point about the theory of knowledge. I think there is a wide range of circumstances in which we find ourselves in a situation for which it is natural to say, "*Well, there are several points of view about this which are pretty much equally rational.*"

So the notion that rationality is itself, as it were, "algorithmic" doesn't answer to a great number of the circumstances where we find ourselves making decisions.

And I think it would be a kind of emotional maturity in us to give up such a picture in morals and in politics and in committees, where we're trying to make collective deliberations and come to a decision.

Questions for Discussion:

1. Do you think rhetorical skills are declining or improving? Do you agree with Howard and Quentin that there may be a link between a decline in rhetorical skills and a lack of tolerance towards other views?

2. How might a mathematician take issue with Quentin's position outlined in this chapter? **Would** *she? To what extent is it reasonable to suppose that there are different types of knowledge—"algorithmic" types that allow for certainty and "moral" ones that don't?*

3. To what extent do our rhetorical skills depend on our current state of technology? If I had an infallible lie detector, for example, how would that influence the rhetorical capabilities of my political community?

4. How might social media be used to simulate various desirable aspects of the Roman rhetorical tradition? Those interested in a discussion of this question as applied to the ancient Greek rhetorical tradition are referred to Chapter 8 of the Ideas Roadshow conversation **Democratic Lessons: What the Greeks Can Teach Us** *with Stanford University classicist and political theorist Josiah Ober.*

VI. Reshaping a Moral World
Recovering important ideas

HB: Let me pick up on the comment that you made a moment ago about going off the rails, and extrapolate from there to another comment that you make towards the end of *Liberty before Liberalism*, where you talk about how you see the role of an intellectual historian.

The analogy you chose was that of being an archaeologist of great ideas, some of which—hence the archaeology reference, presumably—might have been cast aside or forgotten; and you look at it as an aspect of your job as an intellectual historian to re-examine these ideas—to dust them off, as it were—and bring them back to light.

It seems to me that this serves two purposes: to reassess these ideas in light of our recent experiences, and to force us to rethink our fundamental assumptions, or even our recognition that we have made such assumptions in the first place.

Is that an accurate depiction, and do you still look at your role that way?

QS: Yes. That's part of how I see myself. I suppose that I also want to try to make sure that I'm not being philistine about the task of the historian. If I think of the kinds of history that truly matter to me, thinking of intellectual history very broadly, I'm very interested in the history of art and architecture and I have more than a passing interest in the history of music.

If we think of all of these as kinds of history, then—just as historians of literature, where it's a much more familiar thought—we are going to valourize what we study in and for itself. Historians of art in the United States get a better hearing for this than they do in my country. It's a very striking fact how important the history of art is in this country.

And I want to associate myself with a view that it would be philistine to suppose that the point of the past is to help us in some completely utilitarian way. It is to enlarge our imaginations and to enable us to walk through many buildings where we learn things all the time, to get out of ourselves, to get out of our own society, to think in larger ways about all these works of human spirit.

So that all sounds like a pile of clichés—and it is—but we've somehow got to face those clichés and make something of them. And I say that because my work, insofar as it's been about political and moral theory, has commonly been denounced as antiquarian.

That's to say that I'm very interested in the history of moral and political philosophy, but I'm not interested in the history because I think that it's talking about what we talk about now. And it's a very common assumption in certain parts of our intellectual community that the value of the past is, at best, a mirror: we look into the past and we see ourselves.

We see questions that we still ask—and maybe it might be interesting to formulate that question as they did—but basically we're using these people to help us with our questions. As Derek Parfit once beautifully put it, *"We're grave robbers."*

But I am not interested in being a grave robber. I think that the sensibility of the historian is to try to study the past in so far as we can manage—and of course there are huge philosophical questions attached to this—in its own terms, and try to see it from their point of view.

If we do that, then, what I think we *do* find is exactly what you've said: that in our modern culture, and perhaps also in antiquity, we find many paths not taken.

We tend to write history as the history of the winners. We write the history of wars as the history of the winners, but we also write the history of our culture as the history of the winners. But did the winners always deserve to win?

It's a huge question that historians ought to have at the forefront of their mind while working on anything which is a product of the human spirit and intelligence.

So we've talked a lot today about a particular way of thinking about freedom, where I think that we're not the winners. We lost sight of something. And it's quite easy to provide strong historical explanations of *why* we lost sight of a particular way of thinking about freedom and citizenship, but I've come to think that it is deeper and more powerful than what we've currently got on offer. So we ought to be recovering it, we ought to treat it as buried treasure, we ought to be bringing it to the surface, dusting it down.

And when we do, we find that much in the historical text that offers us this moral vision is awful: very sexist, very militaristic. We don't have to take the whole package—

HB: They might be guide-posts or sign-posts.

QS: That's right, yes. They are aids to thinking outside our own box. There's a perpetual tendency in philosophy for us to treat *our* interpretation, *our* reading of certain concepts, as the canonical reading—because it is for us.

And once you begin to doubt our way of thinking about freedom, which I do, you'd start to doubt other things, because many of these terms are interconnected and inter-defined. You'd start to think differently about rights. You'd start to think differently about equality.

So you begin to reshape a moral world for yourself. You're not, of course, replicating a past moral world. You're taking elements from that world which you might not have thought about and are trying to reinsert them into our world.

And I've come to think that that's a very important part of the intellectual historian's task.

Questions for Discussion:

1. To what extent is Quentin's approach to doing intellectual history itself an example of the rhetorical approach of "looking at the other side of the question"?

2. Why do you think that the history of art is more developed in the United States than in the United Kingdom?

3. In what ways is Quentin's position to history significantly different from George Santayana's famous phrase "Those who don't remember the past are condemned to repeat it"? Might it, in fact, be regarded as to some extent an "opposite" view?

VII. Question and Answer
Resisting the lure of the canonical

HB: I may be forcing parallels where they don't exist, but it seems that there's some connection between what you were talking about with respect to rhetoric, and the distinction between the humanities and the natural sciences.

Let me be very concrete and begin with a concrete example that I hope will take me towards the point I'm trying to make.

If you do a poll of people within an academic community, and ask them whether or not they should bother studying Aristotle, you will find widely divergent views depending on their field of study. The philosophers and perhaps political theorists will likely be very supportive of the idea.

On the other hand, if you were to ask a physicist about the utility of studying Aristotle, a standard sort of reply might be, "*Well, that might be interesting historically, but frankly that's a bit of a waste of time if your goal is to become a better physicist.*"

And the reason typically given for this view is that in the natural sciences, objective progress is made towards the (invariant) truth, so there's no need to go back to Aristotle to get his views on a whole spectrum of issues about the physical world that have been so decidedly superseded by other, superior, frameworks over the centuries.

Now consider the humanities. Consider the merit of asking questions such as, *What is social justice? What is freedom? What is the good life?*

The point is that these are questions that have to be continually addressed throughout the ages—not so much because we're not clever enough to find the answer once and for all, like how gravity works, but because you simply *can't* get one unequivocal answer to these questions in principle, because those very questions are defined *with respect to* specific societies, to specific times and places.

Which might suggest, I think, that for someone in the humanities there is a particular onus to do exactly what you are suggesting: to make a conscious effort to investigate past ideas and values so as to bring to light illuminative concepts that might have been forgotten and summarily deemed irrelevant.

In other words, if you *don't* do what you're suggesting—if you don't focus at least some of the time, on "recovering buried treasure"—you are acting more like a natural scientist in the domain of the humanities, falsely assuming that we are making the same sort of law-like progress towards objective truth with a capital "T".

QS: I find those very congenial comments. I would want to go further and say that in this dialectical relationship between us and the history of our culture, we see very many continuities—and we can focus on them should we choose—but I think it's more valuable to focus on discontinuities, for two reasons.

The first has to do with the contemporary state of philosophy, where, despite efforts to undermine it, which you might think have been philosophically convincing, the fact is that conceptual analysis still reigns.

So when it comes to considering the questions about how we should really think about freedom, how we should really think about rights, how we should really think about justice, I've come to feel that the reason we need a historical approach to questions of that kind is because there *is no* canonical reading to be given of these concepts.

Naturally, if we're talking about the idea of freedom, we must in some way be talking about human agency and choice, so we must have some common subject matter, but at some level that's so banal that what's most important is what we erect upon that, what analysis we give of the concept.

What has happened in contemporary political philosophy is that an analysis of the concept, in terms of "negative freedom" and "absence of interference", can certainly be done. And, of course, interference is a very complex notion and so is coercion, so you can do a good deal of detailed analysis: *What counts as coercion? What counts as interference?*

These are not simple questions, so you can amuse yourself for a long time here, but what will **not** emerge is *the* concept of freedom. What will instead emerge is *a* concept, and that can always be confronted with an alternative reading.

Likewise with the theory of rights. It seems to me that we've come to a very strange pass. We're thinking that a right is simply a moral claim. That gives us extremely long and lengthening lists of rights, where the notion that a right might be the correlative of a duty, so that we could say that's a right because we could identify someone whose duty it is that there should be a particular recipient—that's a very different way of thinking about rights. But what makes us think that our way is the canonical way?

There's a perpetual tendency for us to isolate a concept, give it an analysis, and treat that as canonical. Of course, then it fits into all our other ways of thinking.

The role of the intellectual historian in relation to philosophy is to continually try to **denature** these concepts, continually try to make you see that what looks like the necessary might be the contingent.

And some of the most imaginative intellectual history of our time has been done by people who took this approach. Perhaps the most celebrated example of this is Michel Foucault, who famously used the metaphor of archaeology in *The Archaeology of Knowledge*—one of his great texts—to take a concept that you might think *cannot but* be a natural concept and thus *could not* have a history—he chose sex—and then promptly began to write its history.

Of course, the whole thing is socially constructed. *How much of our world is socially constructed such that we have various readings of it, and how much is not?* is a question that he made absolutely central for the human sciences.

But it's remarkable how we've moved back into, as it seems to me, a phase in which we're not very hospitable to that notion. I would like us to be very hospitable to that notion of how much is socially constructed.

HB: Also, once something becomes canonical, not only does it become the only way, tautologically, to look at it; there's naturally a sort of temporal rigidity, so that it's not just "*This is the only way we should look at this now*", but we inevitably drift towards the perspective of saying that this is the *only* way we could have possibly looked at these sorts of things in the past.

QS: Of course.

HB: It seems to me that you're responding to a general tendency out there to, what I would call, "airbrush" history: present a fully-coherent, time-independent view of historical works and events.

In your book *Hobbes and Republican Liberty*, for example, you talk about your motivation to examine the evolution of his ideas through his work, while also explicitly identifying his thoughts as a response to particular societal conditions at the time.

My sense is that you are deliberately humanizing him, that you are steadily determined to move away from this crystalline, air brushed, canonical view that so often seems to befall those in the philosophical pantheon, and are instead explicitly looking at him as a flesh and blood human being who was also a product of his time in an effort to demonstrate the dynamism of his ideas.

QS: Yes. Well, that is exactly the point, and leads on to another of my hobby-horses, but perhaps there are a couple of things I should say about that.

The first comment is simply a little piece of autobiography, which takes us right back to the beginning of our conversation. I'm astonished now by the extent to which, in Wittgenstein's phrase, there was a "bewitchment" by language or concept when I was first writing about these questions about freedom in the Renaissance.

The reason I couldn't make sense of it was that I understood freedom to be in some way the absence of coercion. That was how

I'd been brought up to think about the concept. And so I was thinking, *Well, that's what we mean by freedom, so where's the interference here? I can't make sense of what they're saying.*

Which is to say that I was trying to make sense of what they were saying in the light of a concept that was **not** their concept. And it wasn't until I came to understand their concept from the inside, and contrast it with—as it looked to me to start with—our "canonical" version of the concept, that I really came to think, *Well, we have a pluralism here. We simply do.*

So there is a clear example. Maybe I'm particularly obtuse, but maybe not. Maybe there is a bewitchment by very powerful concepts so that we make them canonical. And we must not do that.

Then the other point you make, which of course connects closely with this, is that the approach I've always tried to adopt as an intellectual historian is to get away so far as possible from the idea of these "deliverances of reason", which we find encased in the books of the very great philosophers. I want to say, "*Think of these texts as interventions in some pre-existing dialogue.*"

There *must* be one. We may not know what it is—and, of course, it's a consequence of my approach that you might find that there's less that you can know than you suppose, so we may never be able to find out whom Plato was really addressing, opposing, satirizing, and so forth. It may not be possible to know him as well as we thought, because you can't know all that by reading the text—you have to know extra-textual matters all along the line to be able to answer questions of that form.

I eventually came to think that these are the hermeneutically interesting questions. So, what seemed to me the interesting questions about Hobbes' theory of freedom in the state are, *Why is he so upset? Who's he trying to discredit? What's the argument? Why this book now? Why does he stop writing his physics in order to write this? What's the crisis?*

You very nicely call that "humanizing" them, but I'm simply trying to supply these people with underlying purposes and motivations.

I'm trying to show you that once you've recovered those motivations then you'll likely understand the text as the text was written.

HB: Wonderful. Anything else? Anything you'd care to add?

QS: Well, that last thought really enabled me to say something about historical method, which is very important to me. This is what R.G. Collingwood liked to call "the logic of question and answer"—don't think of these texts as anything except answers to questions. So, what is interpretation? It's finding out what the question might have been to which the text is the answer. It's an extraordinary illuminous thought, that, I think.

It's not going to be *one* question; and that's why it's going to be so complicated. *What's this person's question? What's the problem? What intervention are they making? Whom are they agreeing with? Whom are they dismissing? Whom are they satirizing? Whom are they ignoring?*

All of these come to the fore—especially, *Whom are they ignoring? Whom are they trying to discredit? Whom are they trying to "airbrush out"?*

So, Hobbes is trying to "airbrush out" the republican theory of freedom. Why? Well, because he thinks that the most successful, and probably the most respectable, form of constitution is an absolute monarchy. Meanwhile, these people have said that the **only** legitimate form of constitution is a democracy. So he's got to "airbrush them out".

HB: Quentin, thank you so much for your time. For my part, this has been a positively enchanting conversation.

QS: Well, thank you very much, Howard. It was a tremendous pleasure. Very skillful.

Questions for Discussion:

1. In a world where no "canonical" measures exist, is it possible to have a Universal Declaration of Human Rights?

2. What do you think that Quentin means, exactly, when he says that the role of the intellectual historian should be to continually try to denature concepts and make you see that what looks like the necessary might be the contingent?

3. To what extent is the temperament for rigorous scholarship in the humanities distinct from that required for scientific accomplishment? Those interested in a broader discussion of this topic are referred to the Ideas Roadshow conversation **The Two Cultures, Revisited** with University of Cambridge intellectual historian Stefan Collini.

Continuing the Conversation

Those interested in getting a deeper understanding of Quentin's thought are encouraged to read his many related works touched on during this discussion, including: *Liberty Before Liberalism, Hobbes and Republican Liberty, Forensic Shakespeare, From Humanism to Hobbes* and *The Foundations of Modern Political Thought*.

Ideas Roadshow Collections

Each Ideas Roadshow collection offers five stimulating expert conversations presented in an accessible and engaging format.

- *Conversations About Anthropology & Sociology*
- *Conversations About Astrophysics & Cosmology*
- *Conversations About Biology*
- *Conversations About History, Volume 1*
- *Conversations About History, Volume 2*
- *Conversations About History, Volume 3*
- *Conversations About Language & Culture*
- *Conversations About Law*
- *Conversations About Neuroscience*
- *Conversations About Philosophy, Volume 1*
- *Conversations About Philosophy, Volume 2*
- *Conversations About Physics, Volume 1*
- *Conversations About Physics, Volume 2*
- *Conversations About Politics*
- *Conversations About Psychology, Volume 1*
- *Conversations About Psychology, Volume 2*
- *Conversations About Religion*
- *Conversations About Social Psychology*
- *Conversations About The Environment*
- *Conversations About The History of Ideas*

All collections are available as both eBook and paperback.

www.ingramcontent.com/pod-product-compliance
Lightning Source LLC
Chambersburg PA
CBHW030903080526
44589CB00010B/121